CONTENTS

Introduction   ix

1   An Early Plan of Action
    HURDLE: Discipline can be an overwhelming task   1
    GOAL: Plan *before* problems arise

2   Disagreements over Discipline   6
    HURDLE: Curbing arguments about raising children
    GOAL: Find harmonious solutions that work

3   Can We Discipline Without Spanking?   10
    HURDLE: Powerful discipline without physical force
    GOAL: Learn which nonphysical techniques work

4   Punishments: Take Time Out, Lose Privileges   16
    HURDLE: How can we make lessons stick?
    GOAL: Consistently stand by a discipline plan

5   Thumb Sucking and Pacifier Use   21
    HURDLE: Should our child have a security object?
    GOAL: Form a satisfying decision

6   The Stubborn Twos   25
    HURDLE: When willfulness yields to temper tan-
             trums
    GOAL: Learn to handle a taxing child

7   Problem-Solving Games   29
    HURDLE: Our toddler ignores our commands.
    GOAL: Learn about words children do not under-
             stand

8   Toilet Training with Ease—and Unease   33
    HURDLE: The bathroom has become a battleground
    GOAL: Toilet train our child without combat

9   Lying—Differences Between Fantasy and Pathology 38
    HURDLE: We seem to need a home lie detector
    GOAL: Raise an honest child

10 Stealing   42
    HURDLE: Our four year old took crayons
    GOAL: Discipline with a long-range point

11 When Kids Fight with Friends or Siblings   46
    HURDLE: Dodging the referee's job
    GOAL: Develop rules to help children settle dis-
             putes

12 Bedtime Blues   50
    HURDLE: Our child will not go to sleep
    GOAL: Devise a bedtime plan that works

13 Crude Language and Name Calling   54
    HURDLE: Our child adores profanity
    GOAL: Clean up our child's language

14 The Difficult Child   58
    HURDLE: Our child seems impossible
    GOAL: Discover *why* discipline fails

15 Toddlers and Chores   62
    HURDLE: Who cleans the mess?
    GOAL: Secure cooperation and good habits

16 Destructive Discipline and Constructive Discipline 67
    HURDLE: Letting anger control you
    GOAL: Learn to be more effective

17 The Family Name   71
    HURDLE: Our child disgraces us in public
    GOAL: Learn when to ignore other people's
                reactions

18 The Guest's Responsibilities   76
    HURDLE: Our friend does not understand children
    GOAL: Set behavior standards for company man-
                ners

19 Rewards   80
    HURDLE: Our child doesn't obey unless we bribe
                him
    GOAL: Use rewards effectively

20 Discipline Helpers Without Rivalry   85
    HURDLE: Trying not to compare brothers and
                sisters
    GOAL: Find methods to boost sibling relation-
                ships

21   How Would You Feel If...   89
     HURDLE: Our child seems insensitive
     GOAL: Teach children empathy

22   Telephones and Children   93
     HURDLE: Our toddler wants to use the phone
     GOAL: Learn about early training for the
               telephone

23   Rules in the Supermarket or the Store   98
     HURDLE: Our child wants to buy everything
     GOAL: Help our child understand limits

24   When Friends' Parents Have Different Rules   102
     HURDLE: Our friends let the children go wild
     GOAL: Help our child learn about differences

25   Apologizing to Our Child   106
     HURDLE: Not knowing when to back down
     GOAL: Discriminate between respect and weak-
               ness

26   Answering Back   110
     HURDLE: Our child wants the last word
     GOAL: Find techniques to settle disputes

27   Dawdling and Forgetfulness   115
     HURDLE: How can we end infuriating habits?
     GOAL: Teach memory and organizational skills

28   Bringing Friends Home   119
     HURDLE: How can we encourage children to play
               here?
     GOAL: Learn social give and take

29 Manners   124
    HURDLE: Our child demands but never says thank-you
    GOAL: Introduce please and thank-you

30 Food Preferences   128
    HURDLE: We make two dinners a night
    GOAL: Arbitrate food preferences

31 Sharing   132
    HURDLE: Can we get our children to share?
    GOAL: Discover when sharing is appropriate

32 Discipline During and After Illness   136
    HURDLE: We think we spoil our child when he's sick
    GOAL: Reinstate the routine

33 Privacy in the House   140
    HURDLE: Our family discussions go public
    GOAL: Learn to speak carefully

34 Aggressive or Passive   143
    HURDLE: Having a child who hits or is a victim
    GOAL: Teach our child when and when not to fight

35 Watching Television   148
    HURDLE: Not knowing what is *too much* television
    GOAL: Learn to manage TV viewing

36 How to Manage When We Are Exhausted   152
    HURDLE: We may make mistakes at the end of the
              day
    GOAL: Set a time-out for parents

37 Who's Right—We or the Experts?   156
    HURDLE: Swaying with the expert winds
    GOAL: Understand demands and depend on
              instincts

38 When to Seek Outside Advice   160
    HURDLE: How do we know if we have a problem?
    GOAL: Develop a checklist to evaluate
              difficulties

Questions and Answers   165

Glossary   169

Resources for Parents   171

Suggested Reading   175

Index   177

INTRODUCTION

As a journalist and a physician, a mother and daughter, we wrote this book from deeply held convictions about discipline, which we learned through observation, research, and practice. Discipline, a journey beginning in infancy, has a goal: to help children achieve their highest potential. Discipline is the series of acts, which, before we know it, form a relationship.

Your choices, decisions, and explanations about discipline can help you raise independent, responsible children who can judge the truth, worth, and wisdom of choices. By explaining and informing and by showing young children how to listen on small points you help them understand about when and why to comply with the larger points. Somewhere along the way, your choices and decisions about discipline blossom into love, understanding, and trust between you and your child. We hope this book helps you forge strong ties.

Many people help make a book possible. We thank Arthur Siegel, the most loving father and husband in the world, who never doubted what we could accomplish. We thank our parents and grandparents, Morris and Gertrude Novick and the late Gertrude and Joseph Siegel, for paving the way. We thank Joan, Mark, and Shana Siegel for participating in endless readings and discussions. We thank countless parents, including Shari Ritter, Laura Siegel, Margaret Shouvlin, Abbe Zuckerberg, and Gaby

Siegel, M.D. for sharing their experiences, questions, and insights. We thank Nancy Schulman, director of New York's 92nd Street Y Nursery School, and Ellen Birnbaum, nursery school teacher, for sharing time and wisdom. We thank Grace Freedson for believing in our idea, and Linda Turner, our editor, for her patience and professionalism.

This book addresses many discipline concerns you will meet while raising your child. Use the keys to reflect how to handle these situations; modify the suggestions to fit your lives, your values, and your child's distinct needs. Consider the material as a starting point to think about discipline or as a chance to exchange views with a friend. To swap advice or information with other parents or to locate services, refer to the directory of parent groups across the United States at the end of the book.

1

AN EARLY PLAN OF ACTION

HURDLE: *Discipline can be an overwhelming task*

GOAL: *Plan before problems arise*

A mother told us a story filled with information about discipline. One evening just before her children went to bed, she remembered their powder paints were still downstairs in the playroom. As she carried the paints upstairs, she tripped. Because the children had not secured the tops, nor had she checked them, the powder floated up in a cloud, settling on the creamy white grass cloth wallpaper and on the blue carpet in her new home. She loved this house, which was everything she ever dreamed of, and she considered the grass cloth wallpaper the topping on a terrific dessert. The paint reddening the wallpaper startled her but did not anger her. She believed she could easily vacuum the mess.

Her attempts to clean the red powder only spread it, staining the carpet and wallpaper. Then, as they say, she lost it. Frantic, she yelled and screamed at her three children, who quietly stared at her. Finally, five-year-old Jake braved the space between screaming sentences, asking if he could say just three things.

She muttered between clenched teeth, "Yes."

1

"First," he said, "you told us no matter how much you yell you still love us."

Still clenching her teeth, she replied this was true.

"Second," he continued—once he squared away the most important point for him—"You told us when we were that angry, we should hit our pillow." Silently she nodded as a smile bubbled inside.

"Third," he said, "Why don't you try soap and water?"

She broke down and laughed aloud to see her five-year-old gravely giving psychological counsel and practical advice. Once Jake diffused the situation, she saw how unpleasantly she was behaving. She brought soap and water upstairs in a large bowl and scrubbed the stain until it faded.

As she scrubbed, she realized she had lost her temper for many different reasons: she was tired, she had had a fight with her husband, and not only was she angry with him, but she worried about his reaction to the red stain on the white wallpaper and the blue carpet.

Once the children were in bed and the carpeting was drying, she replayed the scene in her head. Jake's comments not only amused and surprised her, they also delivered an important message. Her children had memorized their parent's words as they disciplined them, though at times both wondered if they were listening. Her five year old repeated word for word a script she had taught him; at other times his siblings had done the same.

Frankly, she said, she had no idea how comforting her words were until Jake used them on her. She had often explained that yelling does not mean a withdrawal of love. The children were not allowed to punch other people when

2

they were angry—that's where hitting the pillow came in—and frequently she and her husband talked to them about alternative solutions for problems, such as using soap and water to remove red paint.

Because these parents always thought of options, they taught their children to tackle a dilemma by thinking, What else can you do? In the paint incident, the children clearly had many different options. They also had access to their mother, as indicated by Jake's opening statement, "Can I tell you three things?" Only a child whose parents encourage conversation asks this question.

Over the years, like all of you, this mother recalls spending sleepless nights analyzing her children's behavior. She and her husband regularly discussed discipline methods that worked and those that did not. Their choices formed solid guidelines for the children because when they made decisions, they explained their reasoning and values.

With clear objectives, families gain tremendous strength. Although having discipline goals does not suddenly transform your family into the Brady Bunch, it gives parents powerful tools to solve behavioral dilemmas and to develop desired behavior. Parents who do not discipline their children end up punishing them. Punishment, said child care expert James Dobson, is something you do *to* a child; discipline is something you do *for* a child.

Obviously, like this paint incident, life can take us by surprise. We cannot always behave brilliantly, because we must discipline children when we are ill or when we are exhausted, sad, or angry with someone else. In family life, sometimes the enormous demands on each member become similar to the din of horns during rush hour gridlock. Everybody knows there is an obstacle, but no one can move or do anything except hit the horn. After awhile we move again.

To get moving again, we use our resources and information to strengthen and build self-esteem, provide positive feedback, and find the best problem-solving methods. Effective discipline is not a hodgepodge: it is a thoughtful approach to the key events everyone knows will occur.

Effective discipline begins with parents who fearlessly say "no" and introduce rules and limits early. Rules describe our beliefs and expectations for our children; rules teach our children to cooperate with us and then with others. By defining our rules and limits, we help youngsters learn acceptable behavior even as they exert their independence and creativity.

By eight months, psychologists report babies begin to learn self-control over their behavior. The word *begin* needs emphasis. Although children do not take on adult behavior, they learn to inhibit tempting behaviors and to delay gratification. Self-control, or self-discipline, is the backbone of acceptable behavior.

Consider these key points as you plan your discipline strategy:

1. With each discipline decision, try to answer these critical questions:

   - What kind of child do I want?
   - How do I feel when my child makes me feel like less than a perfect parent?
   - In my heart, what actions do I consider important?

2. Everyone wants a child who understands our motives, accepts our judgment, and loves and

obeys us. This child exists only in our imaginations. Even tiny babies misunderstand our motives, defy our judgment, and intensely dislike us for thwarting them as we teach them to behave. Often we must take something away from the child—a potentially dangerous toy—or restrain the child from an activity, such as running into the road. When the child howls, we feel caught between wanting to be kind and needing to be firm, and we doubt ourselves.

3. Remember, children love their parents deeply, they forgive them, and they are resilient.

2

DISAGREEMENTS OVER DISCIPLINE

HURDLE: *Curbing arguments about raising children*

GOAL: *Find harmonious solutions that work*

D
r. Nancy Engel is a New York psychiatrist who treats adolescents. When many problem adolescents and their parents visit her office, she says the parents have a long history of contradicting each other. Just like tiny brushfires that appear moderately threatening, early discipline disagreements between parents can eventually sweep the family out of control. Do not wait until disagreements take their toll.

Discipline discussions should begin even before pregnancy. Beginning a style of communicating early in parenting helps these conversations become an important, ongoing part of your relationship, both as parents and as spouses. One conversation alone just will not solve your problems.

Parents who discuss divergent opinions find the encounter a lot like arguing about politics. Everyone believes his or her view is correct. As the dispute takes on energy, the drive to win rises. During the argument parents call in reinforcements—the memory of the way things were done in their families. Every family is a tiny society in which the inhabitants observe particular customs. Often, people are emotionally bound to the customs they learned within their families before they married; they think these practices are terrific. Small wonder, then, that even folks who seem to have similar backgrounds disagree vigorously, especially over a baby.

The objective of an argument over discipline is to decide what is best for your child. Trying to communicate means trying to hear what the other person is saying. This means asking questions to fully understand exactly what the person is proposing.

When Alice B.'s first daughter was five months old, the baby stopped drinking her formula. Anxious, Alice spoke to her husband. Her idea was to add sweetener to the milk. Her husband disagreed, believing that babies had to learn to drink milk without sweetener. When their daughter was thirsty, he said, she would drink from her bottle. Now Alice recognized that discussing this issue bordered on lunacy, but as she explained, "First-time parents are that solemn about their children and their new role."

The importance of this amusing discussion was that it represented the first discipline problem Alice and her husband faced and they disagreed. Not only was she startled by her husband's entirely different view, Alice disliked it. Although she strongly wanted to reject his opinion, she wondered how, after asking his opinion, could she behave as though his view was insignificant? A bad precedent, she decided. She resolved to try his method. It worked.

Today she says, "I never regretted that decision because that's when we became a team, although we didn't always agree."

These discussions may be time consuming, but the results are worthwhile. As you discipline your child, you and your spouse learn together. It is easier to learn these lessons jointly. Children become angry when they are thwarted, but the most loving act you can perform is to teach them that their behavior has boundaries and actions have consequences.

Children develop security in knowing both parents are dependable. The advantages of sharing the parenting role are many. As Dr. Engel points out, sharing improves communication during adolescence for parents who fully inform each other over the years. Parents who share the parenting rewards, and the burdens, find being a parent more relaxing, and they discover their children benefit from the distinct characteristics each parent offers. Having a colleague in child rearing is both liberating and a source of comfort.

Here are additional key points to help you negotiate your efforts to become a team:

1. Always maintain eye contact. Shut off the television or radio while you talk. Give the discussion your full attention.
2. Disagree away from your children. Everyone benefits if you develop the habit of conducting battles in private.
3. Avoid emotional language and sarcasm. Do not say "You always..." Do not sarcastically ask, "Really?"
4. Do not angrily dismiss the other person's views. Consider the statement, and try to find one point to which you can start to respond so the other person knows you were listening.

5. Give feedback by summarizing the other person's words, so he knows you heard him and understood him.

6. If you truly do not understand the other person's position, ask if she can explain it; try to understand the logic behind the position.

7. Take time. Do not try to "fit in" a talk session. Communication takes time. Your first discussion may not yield a solution; you may need a second discussion because explaining or understanding a "gut" feeling is difficult.

8. Develop trust and a willingness to try the other person's solutions.

9. If one person's notion of eliciting positive behavior appears not to be working, revisit the problem and modify the plan—together.

10. Sometimes one parent has a stronger personality than the other. If you think you lack the verbal skills to win a debate, plan your argument in advance so you know what points you want to cover.

11. Stick to the point you decide to argue about. Do not get sidetracked into another discussion even if you must echo your point repeatedly.

12. You do not need a sophisticated vocabulary. Simple words can help you make your point.

13. Make sure your point has to do with the child, not with some other irritant such as money or the feeling you need more time together. Be honest. If money or time is the issue, then argue about money and time. Do not use your child to camouflage the topic.

3

CAN WE DISCIPLINE
WITHOUT SPANKING?

HURDLE: *Powerful discipline without physical force*
GOAL: *Learn which nonphysical techniques work*

On a hot, humid summer afternoon—the kind of day you hate to be bothered—Arlene P. sat at the condominium pool. Her two-year-old daughter's whining and nagging was as persistent as the sound of cicadas. Finally, frustrated because the child would not "let up," Arlene gathered their belongings, returned to the apartment, and spanked the little girl. Then, exhausted, Arlene sank onto the couch.

Losing her temper and spanking her daughter made her feel worse. She felt more out of control as she wondered how she would discipline her child during the teenage years. "Would I have to use more force as she grew older? I would end up beating her. I needed a better plan. Although I didn't have the vaguest idea of how to proceed, I swore never to spank her again. Never."

Once Arlene made this choice, she tried to learn about other ways of disciplining children so she could make her points without spanking. She also reviewed the times she got angry to understand why she felt like spanking.

To her surprise, Arlene found that a "big action" seemed necessary when her child misbehaved. "It took me awhile to learn disapproval is a powerful weapon because I didn't realize how much approval means to a little child." She also expanded her bag of discipline tricks by creating a discipline game plan with specific goals and various options. "I learned to wing it less," she says, "and I concentrated on thinking: if this...then."

Arlene explored situations that angered her by asking herself, why am I angry now? "One surprise was that often all I wanted was revenge; I wanted to get even for what I thought was bad behavior deliberately aimed at me." She learned that when her child misbehaved, her image of herself as a parent suffered. Because parents are hard on themselves, they interpret bad behavior personally, almost as a sure sign of failing at their job.

Parents also get angry and lose their tempers when they feel overwhelmed, by housework, by friends' and relatives' demands, or by their child. They must learn to ask for help or to devise a strategy for pulling back. When they do not ask for help, they should ask themselves why.

Lucia F., for example, moved from Germany to suburban Connecticut with two small children, nine months apart. During the next lonely year, she permitted and encouraged overnight guests to the point of feeling deluged by everyone's demands. Her memory of working as an au pair for a depressed and neglectful mother of two sad, angry girls stopped her from asking for help. In Lucia's view, only total attention overcame neglect, yet her full-time devotion to her children made Lucia miserable. Once she realized she was different from the mother she had worked for, she hired a baby-sitter for a few hours: she asked for help.

Ann C. could not afford outside help so she placed her children in the crib or playpen where they were safe and then she took a time-out. She headed for the shower each

11

time she felt her anger rising to the point of losing control rather than yield to the urge to spank. "For awhile, I was the cleanest mom around."

Another important discipline goal is to react immediately and consistently, keeping before us the image of building a house brick by brick. Good behavior is learned gradually, mainly because learning and memory are complicated processes in which our child grows to understand our words, our logic, and *how* to do what we want. Telling children "stop that" without giving them other options may be useless.

Since children must repeat tasks often before they learn them, it seems as if they misbehave repeatedly. Exasperated parents often say, "I know he understood because he stopped hitting Janie yesterday. Why is he hitting her today?" It seems like the child opposes us purposely, but children's memories and reasoning abilities are not yet fully developed in the first few years of life. Parents should expect shifting behavior because we transmit so much information every day that, at times, the child is overloaded.

Here are additional key points to consider as you think about a discipline strategy that avoids hitting:

1. Define the behavior you want in terms of exact boundaries.
2. Consider rating this behavior. Do you want your child to get an A for the desired behavior, or can you live with C behavior?
3. Learn about the appropriate developmental abilities for each age so that you do not judge your child by adult standards. Read about the subject. Perhaps start a parent's discussion group, or join such a group.

4. Answer the question, in my heart, what action do I consider important? Sometimes, particularly in public, we are angry because we feel that all eyes are upon us, and in our discomfort we attribute adult views to our little child, thinking of his action as a power struggle. Try to think of his action as an opportunity for a training experience.

5. If you see your child misbehave, deal with it immediately, because when you get to your car or home, your child will not remember the misdeed, nor will she know how to improve her actions. When you reprimand a child, keep a stern, serious face for the count of 10. You are not being mean; you are making a point. Remember children dearly love their parents even when they act as though they hate you.

6. Do not expect the child to obey just because you say "no." Some children might, but others will not. You must convince him you mean business by combining action and voice and removing him from the problem, place or thing. Calling out "no" from your chair communicates to the child that you are not serious; calling out works only after the child repeatedly sees you act.

7. Once your child is past two, warn her about consequences of behavior. Say, "If you continue to behave this way, you will miss your favorite storybook time." Emphasize the word *favorite* to reinforce with your tone of voice that you will take something good away. If you make the consequence sound like a penalty, she will understand.

8. Develop meaningful consequences for children who are three years and older; children younger than three cannot understand the concept of consequences. Consequences do not have to be

the equivalent of calling out the militia. They can be small, mainly because they are meant to illustrate a point and get results. Since you must be able to carry through on a threat, choose only realistic threats. Threatening to break a child's arm is not realistic, but telling a child she will lose a privilege is.

9. Do not try to pretend that you are not the one punishing your child by threatening the child with a third person, such as the other parent or a doctor. Never say, "If you are not good, the doctor will give you a shot." Since doctors do not give shots for bad behavior, you will get away with this lie once or twice. When the child catches on, he'll merrily continue misbehaving. He learns there is no price attached to misbehaving.

10. Distracting children is an excellent form of discipline or training that avoids confrontation, especially with younger children. Before you remove the object the child is playing with, introduce a new object in an enticing way. "Look at this pretty ball." Then, roll the ball back and forth, engaging the child, and remove the other object.

11. Some children will not be distracted; instead, when an object is removed from them, they scream. Make yourself tolerate the screaming. You are not torturing your child, you are helping her learn acceptable behavior.

12. Tell your child in precise words what behavior you expect. Avoid general statements because they only bewilder children. Give your child the option to behave the way you suggested or face a consequence. Say, "You may continue whining if you wish, but if you do, we will leave because you are acting so cranky." Be prepared to carry out

this threat. Once your child knows you carry through on threats, he behaves better with only one warning.

13. Learn to manage your anger so that it does not get out of control. Try to understand why you get angry. Are you in public? Are you exhausted? Are you alone?

14. Remember, the same punishment does not work for all children. Learn to be creative.

15. Do not slap, punch, or hit a youngster hard to make a point. Children want your love even when they are defiant; they can be mortally insulted by only a fierce glare. You can make the point effectively with a soft voice and clear disapproval, a frown, a scowl or a shake of the head.

16. Everyone knows about positive feedback to children, but parents need rewards, too. When your new approach works, offer yourself congratulations, even if you just grin privately and tell yourself what a great job you did.

4

~~~~~~

PUNISHMENTS: TAKE TIME OUT, LOSE PRIVILEGES

HURDLE: *How can we make lessons stick?*

GOAL: *Consistently stand by a discipline plan*

Adele H. and Sandra B., both mothers of little children, recall the difficulties of using time-out as a punishment for the first time. Adele says, "The first time I had to set down discipline, I did time-out and Carol did not understand." Sandra admits, "I got carried away with the idea, and I put him in his room as punishment, but when he tried to leave, I hit him. He screamed because he did not want to stay in his room, and I had to shut the door."

It was a toss-up over who was more out of control: parent or child. Sandra made time-out work for her four year old by changing her approach. "I realized I used time-out to get rid of Michael when he acted up, or I used it as a weapon or revenge for his misbehavior." Instead, she sat with her son in his room, calmly explaining quiet time. Although he could not leave his room, Michael no longer felt abandoned, and time-out became a learning tool, a winding-down time.

Until children are one to two years old, you decide how they behave within the confines of their emotional, physical, and verbal ability. From two years old forward, you want to engage children in a partnership aimed at having them monitor their own behavior when you are not present. Such discipline is not a magic trick; it demands attention, consideration, consistency, and time.

Although a new discipline plan may seem to work quickly, soon children may try old behavior. Do not treat setbacks as a capital crime, and do not give up. Hold your youngster gently, look in his eyes, and firmly repeat the new rule. If the child persists, then warn him: Once more, and...

Be assertive. Aggressive is hitting or yelling; passive is ignoring the behavior, pretending it does not exist. Being assertive requires two statements:

1. "I'm telling you to..." Speak firmly even if you feel like wavering. Children need to believe you are in control.
2. If you get no response, say, "Last chance. Either do this or I will..." Explain the consequences.

Here are suggestions about consequences for little children:

- Remove the object in controversy—"If you cannot play with the blocks without using them to hit, I will take them away until tomorrow." Communicate disapproval by actions, not just words. Convince your child by your facial expression and tone of voice that she has surpassed your limits.
- Use consequences with immediate meaning. Do not threaten to eliminate storytime when it is seven hours away.

17

- Reserve the big guns for a major incident. Threatening to take away story hour may be a huge punishment, especially if this is your special time together. When possible, consider a lesser punishment.
- Choose realistic goals. Must a shy child say hello to a stranger? Is it necessary to show how social he is?
- Consider whether you automatically say "no" often. Sometimes we are so engrossed—when we plan a party, when a family member is ill, when we fight with our spouse or friends, or when we think about work—we do not realize we act indifferently.
- Avoid using time-out if you see your child laughs or if it becomes a game. Sensitive children respond because you disturb their play and they feel punished. Other children may repeat their behavior if you use only time-out without other consequences.
- Avoid battles of will by phrasing questions differently. Do not politely ask, Should we? Do you want to? How about? when you want to choose the answer. Requests give children the option to say "no." When you want cooperation, phrase the question positively, and add a small choice: "We are going to the store. Do you want to take your teddy bear or your book along?" Small choices inform children that no room exists for a discussion about whether to go to the store.

Try to relax and ignore some behaviors. If you minutely inspect every action or treat everything like a national emergency, your child grows up with a negative view of herself—she believes she is incompetent—and she views the world fearfully. "It's hard for parents to overlook behavior because we think if we don't actively *do* something, then we are not being good parents," acknowledges Julie O'Malley, Ph.D., a Pennsylvania family therapist.

Since children hate to stop an activity, transitions cause many arguments. Try an early warning system. Tell your child about the order of events so he understands what to expect. Remind him gently before a visit that it will end at a certain point and he can play with his friend again on *another day*. Youngsters need to learn the concept of again, tomorrow, and another day. In some situations, timers help children switch gears without your raising your voice.

Here are additional key points to consider when you want lessons to stick:

1. Treat your child as a capable and lovable person even as you discipline her. When you express confidence in her ability to behave, it helps her believe in her ability.
2. If you punish a child, tell him you still love him. Imagine how you would feel if your spouse forgot to tell you this.
3. Love is only a meaningless word unless you back it by actions, such as listening, hugging, and praising a child or stopping a child from doing something dangerous.
4. Overact to make a point. Stage actors exaggerate their facial expressions to convey emotions. Sometimes when parents exaggerate shocked surprise, it stops children long enough to distract them or to talk to them.
5. Do not discuss new plans for discipline with friends, spouses, or relatives while the child listens. Discuss this privately.
6. Avoid telling your child that her actions "hurt" you. You can say your "feelings" are hurt or that you are "disappointed" with her actions.

7. If one parent is more of a disciplinarian, do not threaten, "Wait until I tell Daddy (or Mommy)." Instead of concentrating on inappropriate behavior, your child wishes for Daddy or Mommy to disappear.

8. Use books or records with morals, educational TV shows, or an older child, preferably out of your immediate family, to make a point about preferred behavior.

9. Do not order little children into a new behavior or out of a mood. Offer a cold drink to a child who awakens from a nap crying and fussy. Sometimes children are quite thirsty after a nap. Engage him in a toy, a book, or a new way to build blocks. "Look at this puzzle Daddy found. Can you do puzzles? Let's see if we can do this together." Or, "Look at Teddy. Does he want to hear a record?" Distraction is a marvelous instrument.

10. Time-out works only with "time-in," moments when we show children love and attention by kisses, hugs, or watching TV shows together, according to Edward Christophersen, Ph.D.

11. Evaluate whether time-out can work for you, and then plan when and where to use this method. Generally, a location is less important than the way you warn about and enforce time-out. Rather than use a child's room, consider the stairs or a chair not too far from the action. An isolated child may imagine her siblings receive treasured advantages and experiences.

5

~~~~~~

THUMB SUCKING AND PACIFIER USE

HURDLE: *Should our child have a security object?*
GOAL: *Form a satisfying decision*

Before giving birth, Margaret D. insisted her child would not have an "ugly, disgusting" pacifier. When her daughter was seven hours old, however, the doctor suggested a pacifier because "some babies seem to need to suck more than others." In seconds, Margaret tossed aside her opinion, purchasing a dozen pacifiers. She wanted to do what was best for her infant.

Many parents agree with Margaret's decision, but others believe pacifiers or thumb sucking harms the baby's teeth, forecasts permanent immaturity, or signals stress. Whether babies should have pacifiers or suck their thumbs is controversial. Even doctors and dentists disagree. So what can you believe and what should you do?

While trying to develop your personal perspective on thumb sucking, remember the invisible argument behind many parents' strong positions: What will other people think? Worrying about what other people think is risky, especially because other people frequently give you the "party line," the line even they may not believe. Marian and Adam B., for example, decided after long discussion to permit their son to keep his pacifier until he threw it away.

Because Marian was sick for an extended time, Tommy spent several weeks with his grandmother when he was about one year old. Then the family moved into a new house. The one constant in his life was the pacifier.

When Tommy was four, Marian visited the elementary school with him, and the school secretary was shocked when she saw Tommy's pacifier. "Mrs. B.," she gasped, "*What* is that I see?" Coolly and firmly, Marian said she and her husband had discussed it, and they had decided to let him have his pacifier until he gave it up. "I left no room for discussion," says Marian. "Then the secretary confessed to me: 'My son had his pacifier until he was five and he is a school principal.'" Marian laughs when she tells the story, saying, "I don't know who benefited more by my assertive approach, her or me."

The story has two morals: (1) Do not assume other parents have not thought through the pacifier or thumb issue. (2) Do not let others impose views upon you that may not be correct for you and your family. Base your decision about thumb sucking and pacifiers on your instincts about your child rather than on what other people say.

Today we know that sucking is a universal habit: researchers using ultrasound saw how many babies begin thumb sucking in utero. Babies suck from a need to calm, reassure, and satisfy themselves. By answering this need, they take their first steps toward independence.

Sucking a finger or pacifier, most experts agree, is harmless and produces fewer fussy, colicky babies. Both breast- and bottle-fed babies may need to suck a pacifier.

Some parents introduce a pacifier because they believe pacifiers are an easier habit to eliminate than thumb sucking when the child is older. Although no evidence exists on this subject, it may be true because you can slowly remove a pacifier. Studies also show that pacifier sucking does not compromise breast-feeding, according to the American Academy of Pediatrics. But remember, you can try to encourage your child to take a pacifier, but you may have no choice. Some children prefer their thumbs.

Whether they choose thumbs or pacifiers, children turn to comfort objects when they are tired, separated from others, as at bedtime, or feel a strong negative emotion, such as jealousy. As they mature and discover different ways to cope with the stress of separation or their emotions, they gradually reject thumbs or pacifiers.

Some of our fears about sucking thumbs or pacifiers originate from our deepest worries about making mistakes. Mistakes are inevitable. Most fumbles can be corrected with time and thought. Although we influence our children, their psychological health—and ours—is a lifelong struggle, which we neither win nor lose in a single dispute.

Here are additional key points to consider as you evaluate how to handle thumb or pacifier sucking:

1. Do not interpret crying as a sign of hunger. A baby who gobbled down four ounces an hour ago may not cry from hunger but from a need to suck.
2. Helping children learn to tolerate tension is part of the pleasure of parenting. Over time, you see how your actions and words influence your child.
3. Some children turn to sucking because they need a physical release from tension, not because they are more immature or overloaded than another child. Consider introducing physical play and exercise as substitutes for the pacifier or thumb. Gear the physical activity to the child's age, using imaginative play with physical exercise.

4. Many children use the pacifier or thumb to help them fall asleep. Think hard about discouraging them because these children seem to need the extra physical help.

5. Reading irritable children a story instead of giving them a pacifier comforts many children. Young babies, as small as one year, can enjoy a book. They like the physical contact, the act of identifying a bird or cow, and the delight in your eyes as they recognize an object. To the child this is love.

6. If you find yourself totally repulsed by the pacifier or thumb sucking, before acting try to understand why you feel so strongly.

7. Do not try to embarrass a child into abandoning these forms of self-comfort. Embarrassment makes a child feel like less of a person and may create a war around pacifier or thumb sucking.

8. Remember that most children relinquish the thumb or pacifier if we ignore the habit.

9. Talk to your pediatrician about pacifier or thumb sucking if you are concerned.

10. Try to determine which events strain your child. Some strains are unavoidable, yet monitoring may help you lighten the stress load. Sometimes just sticking to a routine soothes a child.

11. Remember these safety tips:

   • Do not tie a pacifier around the child's neck. Children can strangle on the cord.
   • Do not dip the pacifier in honey or syrup. Honey can cause infant botulism in babies under one year, and syrup can produce cavities.

6

THE STUBBORN TWOS

HURDLE: *When willfulness yields to temper tantrums*
GOAL: *Learn to handle a taxing child*

An outing to the zoo illustrates the parent and child misery that can follow an outburst of temper. Breathless and enthusiastic, Betty F. and her husband Henry left their New York City apartment with their two year old in tow. As Betty locked the door and went downstairs to catch a cab, she excitedly repeated, "We're going to the zoo! Isn't that wonderful?" Each time her son gave her a winning smile. Inside the cab, Henry placed Danny on his lap, saying, "The zoo is a great idea, huh, tiger?" Again the child smiled. Both parents contentedly imagined the pleasures awaiting them from this outing.

The day was a disaster.

Oh, little Danny loved the animals at the zoo. But when his parents refused to buy him more ice cream, he howled in rage, screeching so loudly the couple felt as though everyone wondered whether they secretly abused the toddler. To avoid more crying, they bought him the ice cream. Later, Danny also had smaller crying episodes when he missed a step and fell and when the peanuts he fed to the elephants ran out. By four in the afternoon, the fatigued youngster began screaming again, and his exhausted parents gave up and went home, angry and confused. "We tried to make him happy but we all ended up miserable."

Like all of us, Betty and Henry found Danny's temper tantrums intolerable for many reasons. His father explained, "We didn't know exactly how to react, we wondered if all that crying and screaming was normal, we wondered why we bothered to take him on the outing, and we were angry with him for embarrassing us."

Well before the outing, Danny's parents' attitudes and behavior management set the tone. They were often puzzled by how to handle Danny's temper tantrums, which began when he was 17 months old. They did not realize this is a time of physical and mental changes for toddlers, who undergo strong inner urges to gain new skills and independence. At first, his parents slapped his buttocks to shock him and stop him from crying. This did not work: not only did he cry harder, Danny began slapping everyone, including his parents.

During the outing, some of Danny's behavior was set up by his parents because of their overinflated expectations for the outing. They unrealistically expected Danny to appreciate this treat, believing that in return for taking Danny somewhere special, he would behave gloriously, paying a tribute to their generosity. Unfortunately, even for adults, understanding another person's hopes takes pretty sophisticated thinking skills. It is also unfair to put such a price on an outing. Disappointment is inevitable because a child can never attain perfect behavior.

At the zoo, the F.'s began by calmly and reasonably telling Danny he could not have a second ice cream, but then, true to their pattern, they yielded. Danny had shown himself to be stubborn and persistent, and more than once, his crying had influenced his parents to yield. They were more influenced at the zoo because they were publicly humiliated.

One way to handle this was to place Danny in a stroller or carry him away from the refreshment stand, waiting until his crying slowed and then trying to engage him in the animals. Sometimes it is best to let the child howl a bit. You can say something soothing, but you do not have to solve the problem.

As the child slows his crying, help him forget the incident by distracting him. Later, when Danny missed the step, fell, and cried out of frustration, his parents were further agitated and disappointed about their outing. Danny was also miserable. Because the F.'s were quite angry with Danny, they did not try to solve the problem.

Here are additional key points to help you handle your child's temper tantrums.

1. Think of the tantrums, not as a clash of wills, but as training sessions when you can get your point across. The F.'s were not mean by refusing Danny a second ice cream, but in their embarrassment, they forgot they were being reasonable.

2. If you are in a public area, don't worry about what other people think; be considerate and remove the crying child from the scene, if possible.

3. If you are in a supermarket when you tell your child she cannot have a toy, book, or certain foods and she screams, take strength from knowing this behavior will disappear once you succeed in making your point, if you are consistent and credible.

4. If you visit your in-laws and you discipline a child who starts to cry, explain precisely, "We are teaching little Danny that he cannot always have his way. I'm sorry if it makes you uncomfortable, but he'll be fine."

5. If your child has a tantrum, make sure nothing in the area can hurt him.

6. Some children throw themselves on the floor. Ignore this child until she stops crying. Sometimes a tantrum occurs over an incident you feel you can correct. For example, you buy the child a balloon and it flies away. It is sad: be sympathetic, but you do not have to buy another one.

7. Some babies scream harder and stiffen when you pick them up. Do not be put off. Try to let this child cry in your arms.

8. Some children turn blue, even faint; they revive quickly without harm to themselves, but parents are shaken by this behavior. Maddy K. said, "I had read about this kind of tantrum, but when my daughter had one, I panicked. I didn't want to see her faint. Instead, I handed her the object I had taken from her, waited until she drew a breath, and then removed it." Once a child who turns blue takes a breath, she may continue screaming but she will not pass out.

9. Think simple. If you are in a department store during the winter and your child screams, it can look like a temper tantrum, but he may be overheated and uncomfortable. Undress him, and offer him a glass of water.

10. A hungry child can have a temper tantrum. Bring healthy snacks, such as vegetables and fruit, on a long outing.

11. Temper tantrums, a normal developmental stage, usually last only about 10 minutes. If they are uncontrollable, seem unreasonable, or continue past four years of age, talk to your pediatrician.

7

PROBLEM-SOLVING GAMES

HURDLE: *Our toddler ignores our commands*
GOAL: *Learn about words children do not understand*

S ome commotions over discipline arise when a child appears responsive to our words but later repeats his actions. Amanda T. watched Jamie, 15 months, head for the lamp. "I said no. He stopped, looked at me, looked at the lamp, but didn't go near it. I thought, aha! he gets it. The next day he headed right to the lamp; he ignored me."

Words are the tools we use to discipline and to teach problem solving. Often we forget that a young child is a novice at language because she seems to understand *everything* we say. Rather astonishingly, little children misunderstand many everyday words. For example, a group of three year olds attending nursery school for the first time heard their teacher command, "Line up." The bewildered youngsters did not understand what she meant.

Older children show they possess problem-solving skills when they make careful judgments, choose appropriate solutions, and understand the consequences of different choices. To acquire such skills, children must first learn the words, then the ideas behind the words, and that actions have consequences. As children grow, they make connections between words, actions, and consequences.

Sometimes we attribute more understanding to children than they possess, mainly because they have "script" knowledge, the information they learn from participating in daily routines. They comply when we tell them, "Hold still while I put on your socks," or "Take your shoes off when you sit on the bed" because we give them these instructions from the time they are little. When we speak, we also supply more information with body cues and facial expressions. When they do not comply, we show disappointment, a visible or audible consequence of disobeying.

Children can appear to disobey because our instructions seem fuzzy. At times we urge children to be aggressive, not to let a friend hit them, but when a child hits his brother, you charge in, commanding, "Don't hit Jamie." Is hitting all right, or not? If he cannot hit, what is his alternative? Your child may not know. Or you may say, "Don't hit Jamie because you will hurt him." Well, an angry toddler sees no reason not to hurt Jamie.

In another familiar scenario, your toddler grabs a toy from another child. You say, "You can't go around grabbing other children's toys. Would you like him to grab your toy?" The child says, "No." You order her to apologize. Issuing orders is top-down, what-I-say-goes discipline, when you decide the solution: apologize.

Before you intervene and reprimand your child for grabbing, listen to his side of the story or watch what is happening between the children. Avoid jumping to conclusions about their intentions when they misbehave. Put on your detective hat to find out why your child hits, bites, or grabs. Listen to your child carefully. Here are some keys to listening well:

- Do not automatically decide the behavior does not have a cause. Ask her *why* she is acting this way. You may find out she believes she has a good reason for her actions. Present and discuss other ways to deal with this kind of situation.

- Let your child talk until he is finished. Do not interrupt.
- Look directly into the child's eyes as she speaks, so she knows you are concentrating on what she is saying.
- Think about his body language as he speaks. Body language can tell you if he finds it difficult to tell the story or whether you need to ask more questions.
- *Ask* your child, "How do you think you would feel if Tommy hit you?" A question like this helps the child consider other people's emotions. We can become good problem solvers if we understand how other people will react and what they are feeling.

After listening, talk about different solutions. Guide your child by suggesting, but instead of imposing your answers, help her explore alternatives. The idea is to teach her how to think so she can solve problems herself.

"Children who solve problems themselves are more likely to carry them out than if an adult suggests or demands the solution," says Dr. Myrna Schure, Professor in the Department of Mental Health Sciences at Hahnemann Medical College and Hospital in Philadelphia. Schure and her colleague, Dr. George Spivak, wrote *Problem-Solving Techniques in Childrearing*, a training approach to help parents teach children social adjustment.

"Children with good problem-solving skills," says Schure, "experience less frustration and are more likely to succeed because if their first option fails, they can turn to a different, more effective scenario."

Children must seek alternatives to replace their inappropriate behavior, but you do not have to be the referee. Instead, teach them how to *think* about their actions.

31

Good problem-solving skills are the offshoot of understanding language and reasoning that depend upon mastering important words, says Schure. Schure and Spivak believe that by playing games with puppets, and by making up scenarios, children learn how to use the words they need for reasoning. Parents reinforce the meanings of these words by asking children such questions as Why? What else? What? and How would you feel if?

Here are additional key points Schure and Spivak make about the words they say young children must understand to solve problems:

1. Use the word *not* in the context of what *not* to do and whether something is good or *not* good. For very young children, begin the game by saying, "Jane is a girl. She is *not* a boy."

2. Use the words *same* and *different* so that your child learns that hitting and kicking are the *same* idea and both hurt, but asking for a turn is a *different* approach.

3. Use the words *happy*, *sad*, and *angry* so your child learns how people feel, and how feelings can change.

4. Use the word *or* by giving the child choices by saying, We can do this *or* We can do that.

5. Use the words *why* and *because*. These important words teach children cause and effect, linking their actions to consequences.

6. Use the words *might* and *maybe*. These words also teach consequences, and they teach a child to develop alternatives. "What else *might* you do?"

8

TOILET TRAINING WITH EASE—AND UNEASE

HURDLE: *The bathroom has become a battleground*
GOAL: *Toilet train our child without combat*

T he one method Amanda E. used to toilet train her three-year-old son was one no one ever suggested and one she discovered quite by accident!

Early one afternoon, Amanda enthusiastically told her two children she was taking them to a new mall 45 minutes from their home where they would shop and have lunch in the restaurant. On the drive out, the three sang tunes from Sesame Street. Within 10 minutes of arriving in the mall, her son told her he had a bowel accident. She realized it was necessary to take everyone home so she could clean him properly.

"I was furious, but I didn't say a word, mainly because I was struggling to control myself. I think the kids could see the steam coming from my ears as we walked back to the car. We drove home in silence. Inside, my five-year-old daughter stopped me. 'Don't yell at him,' she begged."

"'Oh? What should I do?' I asked because obviously whatever I was doing wasn't working, and I was rather charmed by her effort to protect her brother. Her solution: 'Just tell him he shouldn't do it again.' Well, by now I was exhausted, so I went into the bathroom and I said in a dry, emotionless voice, 'Sam you shouldn't have done this.' That was all I said." But from that moment, Amanda reports, Sam never soiled or wet his pants again.

Inadvertently, she discovered the perfect teaching method: ARMM, an acronym for attention, retention, motivation, and motor skills, learning theories suggested by psychologists Bandura and Walters, who researched how children acquire information and behavior.

In this instance, toilet training had Sam's full *attention* because he knew he was in trouble on that ride home. He wanted to *remember* what his mother had been saying about toilet efforts because he was unhappy over the episode. He was *motivated* to control himself because his mother did not lose her control, keeping the focus on Sam's behavior and leaving him with no one to be angry with except himself. Also, Sam had the *motor skills*: he knew what to do, and he knew how to use the toilet.

Toilet training is that magic moment when a child delays bowel movements or urination until he reaches the potty or toilet. Although much disagreement exists about the age at which toilet training must (or can) be accomplished, many parents want their children trained as early as possible because some U.S. nursery schools do not admit children unless they are trained, primarily to prevent outbreaks of infectious diarrhea and hepatitis A.

Culturally, the age at which a child is trained varies. East African Digos, for example, expect their children to achieve bladder control by 12 months. They achieve this goal by initiating training within the first few weeks of life and by paying close attention to the infant's physical cues.

In our culture, understanding your child's physical cues can have important payoffs, not in the first few weeks of life, but later. About four weeks after Elise G. and her husband introduced a potty to their 20 month old, they noticed their daughter was awakening with a whimper at four in the morning. Speculating the child wanted to avoid wetting her diaper, they put their little girl on the potty at once. She performed, and she never wore diapers to bed again. This is an unusual example, because daytime dryness generally occurs first, illustrating that many exceptions can occur during toilet training. With this child, daytime dryness and bowel training followed more slowly.

Your child is ready for training if you observe the following:

- He stays dry for longer periods of time during the day, a sign of better bladder control.
- She wants to be changed out of dirty or wet diapers.
- He gives some sign when he is having a bowel movement, like squatting or grimacing.
- She can pull her pants up and down.
- He has bowel movements on a fairly regular schedule.

Once you see these signs, here are additional key points to consider when planning your toilet-training approach, among them some tips from a symposium on behavioral pediatrics:

1. A potty has great advantages over a toilet because children sit comfortably on it, and eventually they use the potty independently because it is not as high as a toilet seat.

2. Prepare your child for toilet training by introducing the potty and talking to her about it. As you change her diaper, rather than saying she is dirty, point out you are changing her because she is wet

or because she pooped. Before long she will understand the words and ideas.

3. When you approach the actual training stage, take a cue from international diplomats who participate in negotiations with high stakes without showing emotion. Work hard at masking anger or disappointment.

4. Do not attack the subject of toilet training too bluntly. Most children react better when approached indirectly, allowing them to make their decision and take responsibility. Start by telling your child a story about a youngster who was proud of learning how to use the potty. Excellent books and records are available that teach this indirect approach.

5. Battles occur not because your child is stubborn—he may be stubborn—but because you overreact. Often parents consider negativism or setbacks as a personal affront. Take nothing personally, and keep your eye on the goal by enduring the mistakes and hiding your displeasure.

6. When your child performs, reinforce her behavior with praise including: "This is wonderful. Daddy (Mommy) is so proud of you for..." Explaining why you are proud is important, and so are hugs and kisses.

7. Try to have fun. Be enthusiastic and happy about what the child is trying to accomplish so that your attitude becomes contagious.

8. Tell others about the child's triumphs. Children love this indirect praise, and it helps reinforce their achievement so that they develop confidence that carries over to other aspects of growing up.

9. Do not try to train your child when he is ill or if you recently had a new baby or moved to a new home. Both of you will be under subtle emotional pressure, and learning to adapt to two experiences is a lot to ask from a little child.

10. Keep your instructions short and simple. Tell your child to do one thing at a time, not several things at once, and use gestures to further explain what you want.

11. Do not leave your child alone on the potty for an extended length of time, or your child will feel isolated, even rejected.

9

LYING—DIFFERENCES BETWEEN FANTASY AND PATHOLOGY

HURDLE: *We seem to need a home lie detector*

GOAL: *Raise an honest child*

Kerry T. walked into her living room and immediately spotted the can of Play Doh on the carpeting. "If you have two children, and one is a baby, and you find Play Doh in your living room, and no other visitors have been in your home, you don't have to be Columbo to know who left the Play Doh in the living room," says Kerry. Kerry found her three-year-old daughter and asked her, "Did you leave the Play Doh in the living room?" Jill shook her head in denial.

In her anger, Kerry labeled Jill's behavior as lying, since she had warned Jill not to bring the sticky clay into the living room. Children are not born liars, and they do not lie to be harmful or because they are crafty, manipulative, or cunning. Small children lie mainly for four reasons:

1. A fear of punishment
2. A strong desire to satisfy
3. A talent for imitating adult behavior
4. A wish to make something he believes come true

Jill knew she had made a mistake, and her fear was underscored when her mother needlessly asked her, "Did you?"

If you know the answer, avoid trying to trap the child in a lie. In a situation like this, first address the deed—no Play Doh allowed in the living room—and then the lie. Be direct. When you ask a child why she left the play material in the living room, she generally has no answer.

Instead say, "I have asked you not to leave the Play Doh in the living room or play with it there, but today you left the Play Doh there. That means you cannot use the Play Doh for two days." Two days is a long time in a child's life, and the idea behind punishment is to impress upon your child that not following the rules—keeping the clay out of the living room—has consequences.

If your child lies to you, do not use time-out, use time-in. Initiate a conversation about lying. Perhaps explain you will be angrier at your child for lying than for the misdeed, or tell your youngster the story of The Boy Who Cried Wolf. The idea is to teach children that when they lie, people will mistrust them, and if it happens repeatedly, no one will believe them.

Try to discover whether your child understands what fibbing, lying, or pretend means. A child who insists he has just seen Batman may be expressing a wish to see Batman. Gently say, "Batman is make-believe, right?"

Sometimes children lie because they sense the answer you want. They tell you what they think you want to hear. A mother who wants her child to achieve in school may continually press him with questions about whether he knew the answers to the teacher's questions that day, and the child may lie to give the "correct" answer. Inadvertently the parent sets up a situation in which a child learns to lie.

Children also imitate lying behavior. They hear adults around them lying to other adults, and they reproduce the behavior. Or they discover their parents have lied to them. If you tell your child the store is "out of" those toys rather than face a temper tantrum, at some point you lose your credibility and then eventually you lose your child's trust. Adults can differentiate between white lies and real lies, but young children cannot understand subtleties.

Children's trust in us is the key element that enables them to tell the truth. One mother heard her infant son screaming and ran into the bedroom where the baby's older sister was standing rather guiltily by the crib. "What happened?" asked the mother. "I bit him," was the simple reply.

Once she counted the baby's fingers, the mother struggled to mask her anger with the older child and her fear about how easy it was for the older child to inadvertently harm her brother. But this mother thought, "She did tell me the truth. If I lecture, yell, or even spank her for telling the truth, I just may teach her to lie."

Instead, the mother carefully explained the rules of the house: The older child could dislike the baby, even hate the baby, but she could *never* physically hurt the infant. The mother then directed the girl to return to the room, alone, and apologize. The purpose of sending the child to the room alone was to signal trust.

For parents, truth telling often takes much energy because your child may not like your answers to her questions. If we suspect she may act out by crying, it is tempting to lie. To create a close, trusting relationship with your child, parents must tolerate some scenes, not take the easy way out; let children in on your thinking with short explanations.

Here are additional key points to remember when dealing with lying and a young child:

1. Consider a lying episode as a gateway moment, when you can enter and establish the groundwork so that your child will grow up truthful.
2. Do not label children as liars, since they try to live up to their labels instead of changing their inappropriate behavior.
3. Be careful about the kinds of discussions about fibbing that occur in front of children, such as "I won't tell my wife (husband) how much I spent on . . ."
4. Do not participate in cover-ups that teach children to lie. For example, do not say, "We are going on vacation, and we will take you out of school, but we are going to tell your teacher you were sick." Such a story makes school seem less important and encourages lies to reach your ends.
5. Overhearing children lie to make themselves look good in front of parents or peers is not cause for a public discussion. Deal with it later.
6. Do not make children feel worthless or despised if you punish them for lying. Good discipline promotes change, not bad feelings.
7. Being defensive too often may be a clue that you should consider what people are telling you. It is one thing to have faith in your child and another to hide your head in the sand.
8. Rehearse your reactions to a lie before an incident occurs, so that you think through the issue.

10

~~~~~~

STEALING

HURDLE: *Our four year old took crayons*
GOAL: *Discipline with a long-range point*

One wintry afternoon, Meg S. took her child to the drugstore. When they returned home, she pulled off her snowsuit, hat, mittens, and boots. As she put away the clothing, she saw her four year old sitting sadly on the steps. Meg asked the child what was wrong. Looking miserable, the youngster said, "I took something from the drugstore." Promptly Meg said, "Well, we have to return it." Back out came the snowsuit, hat, mittens, and boots. When they were re-dressed, they got back into the car. Driving along, Meg asked the four year old, "By the way, what did you take?"

The child held up an elastic band. Meg restrained herself from laughing. "What stopped me was realizing Ann had assigned a moral value to her actions; the monetary value was unimportant. Ann believed she had done something wrong."

When Meg reached the drugstore, she went to the owner and said in a serious tone, "Ann has something she wants to return." Then Ann held up the elastic band and returned it to the pharmacist, who did not laugh. He understood the point Meg was making.

Sooner or later, many children take something that does not belong to them. Even if you react well, as Meg did, you may not stop the behavior with one response because children are figuring out the world, and they often do not learn a lesson the first time, so we must guide them through the appropriate behavior again.

Finding out that your child stole something does not call for a time-out punishment. Instead it calls for initiating a conversation about property ownership, explaining that often we want something badly, but we cannot take it. In the early years, we teach the rule: We expect you not to steal. Performing the way we want them to is not all we ask of our children, however. We want them to understand the reasons for these expectations, how people are hurt by stealing, financially or emotionally. Explaining that stealing deprives someone else teaches them to have a well-grounded sense of property rights.

After school one day, Erika T. discovered her five-year-old son had a new box of crayons, one she had not purchased for him. When she asked where the crayons came from, he admitted he had taken them from another child's locker.

"I didn't ask him why he had done it. It seemed counterproductive. I knew he had taken them because he wanted them, so I talked to him about the difference between his property and someone else's."

Erika's lesson "took" mostly because she and husband, Ted, modeled honesty for their children. When automated teller machines first opened in Massachusetts, Ted went to the bank and the machine fed him $10 extra. He returned the money to the bank with a note, and the bank rewarded his behavior by sending him a tie and later a small statue, representing the bank's logo. Honesty was a hot topic in this household, and a value. As it unfolded, the family discussed the episode. Our behavior supports or provides evidence about what we believe, more than what we say.

Our behavior and beliefs are more important than words because our children reach their conclusions independently. We want them to think, and not behave as robots following rules, but as individuals who understand and evaluate actions, emotions, and situations. So if you discover that your child stole something, do not think of the punishment. Think of beginning a conversation.

Here are additional key points to consider when you think about discipline for stealing:

1. Your handling of this event depends on how you perceive this issue. Evaluate your opinions.
2. If you discover that your child stole something, be careful not to overreact. This is not his entry into the criminal world. Although stealing should not be treated lightly, overcorrecting by harsh punishment serves only to alienate the child. Children under six do not understand stealing as older children or adults do.
3. Your goal is to help your child develop impulse control and to help her learn why the behavior is inappropriate. You also want him to learn to ask permission, not just take something.
4. You may not be the first to learn about your child's stealing. Someone—a teacher or a friend—may tell you about it. Do not assume this person is correct, but also do not become defensive. This is not a critical review of your parenting but a chance for you to teach your child something important.

5. If you must confront your child, try asking this way: "Monica's necklace is missing and Mrs. G. thinks you may have taken it. Did you?"

6. If your child admits taking the necklace, praise him for telling the truth before discussing the implications. If he denies it, give him the benefit of the doubt, but press a bit. Do not search the child. Let the child think about whether he wants to tell you. He may say he "found" the necklace. Make the distinction for him between ownership and taking someone's property without permission.

7. Little children are not adept at hiding information, so press cautiously. With careful monitoring and probing, the truth emerges slowly. If your child insists she is honest, however, at some point you should believe her.

8. Do not expect to stop stealing with one perfect response. Teaching values requires repetition.

9. If your child steals, ask yourself whether you have overindulged your child to the point where he cannot manage being denied.

10. Sometimes a child steals if she feels neglected, if she feels she is treated unfairly, or if her parents are too domineering. Such children need a chance to make decisions, they need praise, and they need to feel they are important to everyone in the home.

11

WHEN KIDS FIGHT
WITH FRIENDS OR
SIBLINGS

HURDLE: *Dodging the referee's job*

GOAL: *Develop rules to help children settle disputes*

Amanda T., two, pulls other children's hair as hard as she can. John H., three, screams when friends touch his toys. Sherry L., two and a half, pushes and hits her brother when he comes near her toys. What these children share, despite their age differences, is their forceful approach to problem solving when they are angry, overstimulated, or frustrated. Puzzled, exasperated, and baffled parents ask, Does it have to be this way?

The answer is yes initially, because little children have not yet learned alternative solutions. Parents can guide and change their children's behavior, sometimes quickly.

Sometimes fighting stops if the child feels you will protect his rights. He needs to believe in your fairness. Younger siblings, even when they are loved by the older sibling, can be frustrating. Try building a block tower and then let the baby knock it down. You feel angry with the baby also. In this situation, the older child needs protection, a new strategy to cope with his frustration, and insight into the situation. He needs to know the baby's action is not intended to harm his activity.

Children fight in many other situations and for many different reasons. Here are some key moments when you may find your child acting out:

- A young child who has not yet learned to talk may pull hair if she says "Hi" to another child who does not respond. Usually once your child learns to talk, she does not need this strategy. If you think this may be the issue with your child, it is wise to avoid overreacting to hair pulling. Tell her it is wrong, take her hand away, but do not smack her. She may begin to think of smacking as an alternative.
- Many parents find television watching stimulates aggression. One tactic is to monitor TV programs for their contents or eliminate TV for a short period. Mary L. reports that forbidding TV for days at a time restored her son's peaceful nature. She had to punish him this way periodically.
- Make sure your child gets enough physical exercise. On rainy days, he can jump in place, tumble on a mat, or dance to a record. Physical exercise is an important outlet for children.
- Overscheduling can fatigue young children, who act aggressively when they are tired and irritable.

Here are additional key points to consider when you encounter children who are fighting:

1. If your younger child is frustrating the older child by annoying her when she plays quietly, think about using a gate to block the bedroom or part of the playroom. Let the older child play inside the

gate, and keep the younger one outside with many of his toys.

2. It helps to delicately scold the younger sibling even if he is very young because your attitude toward his wrongdoing reinforces the notion that you protect your older child. In a soft, but firm tone of voice say, "No, Andrew. You are not allowed to pull apart Tony's blocks." Your older child then understands that justice is served; the baby may be puzzled, but not agitated.

3. Sympathize with and explain to the older sibling, "It's frustrating to have him knock down your blocks, but he is not as big as you are, and he doesn't understand how to play yet. You will have to teach him." Hug and kiss your youngster to reinforce your love.

4. Do not wall off the older sibling for an entire day if you use the gate approach. Allow time during the day when the older sibling must play with the younger one. She can roll a ball with him or make faces, but it is important to have some interaction so the older child shares with the younger sibling.

5. Give an older sibling a teaching role. It is an important role, and when given this responsibility, he can do it well. He also learns the pride of accomplishment.

6. Ask for feedback from caretakers: you may be working hard at preventing arguments and fighting, yet you may not see great behavioral changes. Children tend to fight more with parents around than they do outside the home. Caretakers or friends may report that your children care for each other quite a bit.

7. When young children see that their parents are fair and protect their rights, they become more

generous instead of focusing on their anger and their frustration.

8. Do not expect siblings to share every possession.

9. You need not interfere every time children fight. If you avoid the referee's job, then children take responsibility for solving the problem.

10. Some children's fights are a way of getting parents to interact with them. Rather than referee, consider fun activities with your children that have nothing to do with taking sides.

12

~~~~~~

BEDTIME BLUES

HURDLE: *Our child will not go to sleep*
GOAL: *Devise a bedtime plan that works*

A s a physician, Beth G. felt guilty about her nights away from her infant. She compensated for her guilt by rocking her eight-month-old daughter, Susan, to sleep when she was home. Both mother and daughter enjoyed this intimate but time-consuming routine. Lewis, Susan's dad, didn't enjoy this routine because he put Susan to bed more often. So the couple decided to end this practice, an effort that Susan resisted by angrily howling.

Bedtime resistance is your baby's first response to separation. Conflicts arise because parents act unsure, mainly because their crying child evokes compassion and concern. Among the bedtime questions parents raise are, Should we stay with our child until he falls asleep? Should we let her sleep in our bed? Should we let him "cry it out"? Because clear-cut answers are not available, parents often act inconsistently, intensifying bedtime separation. Bedtime issues arise from three key causes:

1.   Your child's inability to relax and let go of tension
2.   Fears your child experiences about separation
3.   How much your child feels he can control you

Beth G. and her husband solved their bedtime problem using a progressive delay method devised by Richard Ferber, M.D., director of the Center for Pediatric Sleep

Disorders in Massachusetts. The G.'s placed their daughter in her crib, said goodnight, and let her cry for 5 minutes, using a timer because the sound of her crying "was so awful." After 5 minutes they returned to her room, hugged and kissed her without taking her out of the crib, and then firmly but nicely told her she had to go to sleep. When they left her room, they let her cry for 10 minutes, by the clock.

They returned and went through the same routine, but the next time they let her cry for 15 minutes by the clock. Although Susan was asleep then, parents are told they can return to the room every 15 minutes until the child is asleep. The G.'s reported the technique took two days.

Sometimes parents must manipulate even a good solution when they have a strong-willed child. Rob and Lynn R. hoped to avoid bedtime problems with their second daughter, remembering the difficulties of getting their first daughter to sleep. When their second child was six weeks, however, she developed a serious respiratory infection, and they stayed with her to monitor her breathing. Once the baby recovered, she wanted her parents around at bedtime. When they tried to let her "cry it out," she forced herself to vomit, which some children can do.

The R.'s were told they could leave their daughter in her vomit without doing her any harm, but that idea was repugnant to them. Yet after nights of dozing on the floor beside the crib, Rob admits he was ready to do almost anything to get his daughter to sleep.

When they tried progressive delay, they faced quite a battle. Their daughter did not vomit, but she screamed and threw her toys, blankets, and pillow out of the crib.

In the long run, their efforts were partly successful, mainly because they decided to tolerate some bedtime bad behavior. They worked out a compromise so that Lynn and Rob share bedtime duty. "Now she lets me put her to sleep and I don't stay with her as long as he does. He wouldn't leave until she was absolutely snoring." Some of Susan's improved behavior is a result of maturity and comprehension. She does not vomit anymore or scream at bedtime. Occasionally she still throws her toys out of the crib, but she finally gives up and falls asleep.

At times, bedtime difficulties can arise because we bend the rules in a different setting, such as a hotel. Rhonda and Jerry T., for example, traveled with their son Jason to Niagara Falls shortly before his second birthday. Since he had never slept in a bed alone, they allowed Jason to sleep with them in the hotel because they thought he was frightened. When they returned home, he wanted to continue sleeping in their bed.

Sleeping in a parent's bed has become a debatable notion lately because of a resurgence of literature supporting such behavior. Many parents want their child in bed with them, but equal numbers of parents disagree.

Here are additional key points to remember as you work out a bedtime problem:

1. Parents are sometimes trapped in bad situations because they are tired and unwilling to have a scene. Consider this: If you spend even two weeks curing this problem, think of how many evenings you will spend pleasantly.
2. Be prepared for disruptions of even the best-planned routine. An established bedtime routine from the beginning helps, but it does not take much to disturb it. Overnight guests, illness, a long outing, or staying at a hotel can upset

routines. If this occurs, remember that restoring the schedule can take longer than one night.

3. Initiate a quiet time before bedtime to help your child relax and unwind. Lullabies and reading a story both help to set the mood for bedtime. Establishing a routine for young children is important. They get their pacifier, they get a story and they get kisses and hugs; the same events happen each night.

4. Don't put a bottle in the crib to quiet your child. Liquids with sugar, including milk and formulas, can erode the teeth. Children who drink while they are lying down are prone to ear infections.

5. Consider changing naptime or bedtime, because children sleep better when they are truly tired.

6. Many parents kiss their children goodnight and quickly leave the room; others stick around because they enjoy the cuddly, quiet time. Children are irresistibly sweet then. Be consistent about how long you stay.

7. Be flexible. Sometimes children bring up a topic that worries or interests them when you want to walk out of their bedrooms. It can be important to stay and talk.

8. It is much harder to enforce a new habit once children are two years old, but you can succeed if you are consistent, kind, firm, and loving, and you have a plan. This helps you feel more in control; indecision makes us feel angry.

9. With older children, you can set limits. Set a realistic bedtime that fits the child's internal clock. If a child goes to sleep later than you believe wise, see if he is waking tired and difficult. If he is, he needs more sleep; if he wakes peppy in the morning, he is getting enough sleep.

13

CRUDE LANGUAGE AND NAME CALLING

HURDLE: *Our child adores profanity*

GOAL: *Clean up our child's language*

The salesman waiting for the elevator in the apartment house remarked he had never seen such a pretty little girl. Dark-haired, green-eyed, three-year-old Amy H. wore a ruffled pink dress. Chattering happily, suddenly without missing a beat she looked at the salesman and said, "Oh, F—k. I forgot my doll upstairs."

This put Amy's mom, Christine, over the edge. "I had been trying to ignore the word Amy started using after hearing a friend say it. I hoped she would forget it. But it was clear I now had to talk to her."

Young children are drawn to curse words and name-calling because of their great interest in language. Children understand something important about language. When three-year-old Amy was informed she could no longer use the "F" word, she wailed, "But mommy, nothing else *feels the same*." Certain words do have a feel to them—otherwise none of us would curse. Yet parents need to set rules for verbal aggression, verbal release, and verbal labeling.

Children need not rely on curse words to express themselves. Do not underestimate a child's ability to be creative with language. One five-year-old boy called his mother "stupid." Janet M. lectured her son and she said firmly, "You are not allowed to call me stupid. Never. Never. Never." Yes, her voice rose a bit. The little boy listened intently and he left the room.

Janet said, "He was gone for at least a half an hour in his room. Then he came downstairs where I was working and he asked me a math problem. I said I didn't know the answer, but I could look it up."

Slowly, steadily, never taking his eyes from hers, he replied, "I know what I *can't* call you. But I *can* call you brain-robbed." When faced with not being allowed to call his mother stupid, he had plotted his revenge, inventing a creative way of calling her stupid.

Generally children younger than five comply when parents simply request them not to curse. But be prepared. They may ask you why they cannot use the word or what the word means. Sometimes such requests do not occur privately. It is perfectly acceptable to say, "I will explain later," or simply say firmly, "It is not a nice word," without giving an explanation.

When children use crude language, parents can use the event as an opportunity to initiate discussions about "our family rule." Explain to your child that "in our family, we try to think of ways to express our feelings without using these words."

Name-calling, which is harder than crude language to stop with a request, represents a good chance for parents to introduce discussions about empathy by talking about how another person feels when he is called a name. You also can ask, "How would you feel if someone called you..."

In his book, *Smiling at Yourself, Educating Young Children About Stress and Self-esteem*, Allan Mendler, Ph.D. notes that older children who call others names and act mean are "feeling bad inside and they need others to make them feel good." He suggests helping children practice saying positive things to the other child when they hear put-downs. For example, if one youngster jeeringly says, "You buck-tooth ugly mouth," your child can reply, "You're right. I have buck teeth—but your teeth are beautiful." This approach may be more practical as children get older.

Be careful about jumping to conclusions and over-reacting if someone tells you that your child used crude language or called someone a name. It is more helpful when you get a second-hand report to ask the child questions. Ask your child what her reasons were for calling the youngster a name. Give your child time to explain her side, especially since name-calling, for example, can result from provocation that you did not witness.

Here are additional key points to consider when trying to clean up your child's language:

1. Children use curse words they overhear, no matter who says them, without understanding the subtleties of using such language in private but not in public.
2. When a child first uses crude language, it can be fairly amusing and tempting to wait and see if the child forgets the new word, but usually he does not, so you might as well set the rule immediately.
3. Be careful of the language you use when you are around your children because it is difficult to stop children from using language they hear at home.

4. If you know the crude words the child uses did not come from you or your spouse, ask the day care professionals about expressions that are used at day care. One mother reported that the au pair from another country used a term that was socially acceptable in her country but inappropriate for U.S. children. Once the parent made the au pair aware of the differences, the problem was easily remedied.

5. Crude language is rampant on network and cable television. Monitor the programs your child watches, and listen to the language. Discuss other ways to use language and express ideas.

6. The child who calls other children names may be trying to act maliciously. Ask yourself what is provoking her anger. Sometimes families are preoccupied, and without meaning anything awful, they push the child aside for awhile. This can make a child angry enough to tease other children.

7. If you try to help your child learn to defend himself by telling him the time-honored defense, "Stick and stones can break my bones but names will never harm me," be sympathetic. Being called names is troubling to a child.

8. Be sensitive to the literal child, who may consider a name that someone calls her an accurate indictment.

9. Think of ways to build your child's confidence so he believes he is a worthy person who should stand up for himself with dignity and pride. Make your child feel worthwhile by telling him you love him and by praising him. Help your child know you think you are worthwhile by not permitting him to curse you, insult you or act rudely toward you.

14

~~~~~~

THE DIFFICULT CHILD

HURDLE: *Our child seems impossible*

GOAL: *Discover why discipline fails*

W hen her daughter Karen was four years old, and her son Michael two years old, a friend asked Jane S. when she planned to have another child. A second friend overheard the question. She whipped around, providing the answer: "How can she? She has Michael."

Michael was well-known among Jane's friend as a "difficult" child because he was unpredictable, apt to climb on a counter and open cabinets. He was unterrified by risk. Parents consider other children difficult if the youngster is strong-willed, defiant or whiny or if the child does not meet their expectations.

Such children just do not respond to discipline according to the way experts insist they should or the way more tranquil children do. These children need their parents to create a discipline plan and stick to the strategy for weeks. Parents also need to put in effort to make sure their children understand what is expected of them.

Discipline fails if we find a new technique and give up on it too quickly. Often the child improves temporarily until he finds a new way to try the old behavior again in much the same way that dammed water finds a new opening.

If the new method fails after three tries, we think the technique is a failure, but changing your child's behavior is not easy or quick. If you say, "I have tried everything," consider whether this is the problem: trying new plan after new plan. Do not give up after three trials; form *one* plan and stay with it for a few weeks.

Strangely, too, obstinate children often behave in ways to annoy and alienate you even while they need you to demonstrate great love for them physically and with discipline. It's almost like being on a diet and eating chocolate: you know you shouldn't but you just can't stop.

In Michael's case, Jane was not annoyed, but she was too permissive because she found him interesting, a challenge. Amused by the way his brain worked, she continually laughed about his escapades. Although she prevented Michael from hurting himself, Jane never let him know behavior had limits until her husband Tim turned to Jane and warned, "If we don't do something about him, he will end up in reform school."

Setting limits for Michael wasn't easy. "I'd have preferred going to South America on a secret mission for the CIA," says Jane. Tim agreed. They found Michael complex; his thoughts and actions were contradictory. At two years, he would fearlessly have jumped into the deep end of a pool if you told him to, yet he was startled by loud noises and he was extremely attached to Jane and Tim. Like other children, he hated having limits on his behavior, and he protested by screaming, crying, or whining.

One day Tim just looked at Michael and said, "I love you, but I just can't stand your whining." Jane reported the whining stopped for that day. Children need to be told repeatedly that you love them and explicitly which behavior you do not like.

59

Together they worked lovingly with him, but disciplining Michael took great energy and concentration. "Mostly it wasn't what we did that worked," says Jane. "It was saying no to him, meaning no, explaining what we wanted, and staying firm. It's like tennis: you can never lose your focus."

Behaviors like whining irritate and tax parents. Whining can last until a child is older or more mature or until parents become firm and decisive. If you try to ignore the whining child, you can be guaranteed their maddening behavior will reach the point at which you snap. Because you are so angry, discipline is impossible, and so is a good relationship with this child. Yelling or asking a child to stop whining generally fails. Children do not sense when they start whining, so they can't understand how to control it. When your child begins to whine, take his hand and gently say, "You are whining. Please ask in your regular voice." If you imitate the whining, do not try to shame your child but try to teach him the difference in the sounds.

Parents object to whining for its grating sound and because they hate being manipulated by the child. Whining is a call to action that starts when we tell our child "no." If you decide to take a strong stand when your child whines, then warn her about the impending change. Explain the new ground rules carefully and precisely.

Here are additional key points to consider when you wonder why discipline seems to fail with a difficult child:

1. Ask yourself whether your child has traits like you. Sometimes we respond poorly to the child who is just like us because we know our flaws all too well. At other times we respond poorly to a child who is unlike us because we simply don't understand him. When we understand why we

respond to a child in a certain way, we can help ourselves.

2. By understanding our negative reactions to the child's behavior, we can avoid disagreements. Instead of thinking *oppose*, think *change*.

3. Even if you can change your child, you will not accomplish this change overnight. You are in this role for the long haul. Do not try for a 100 percent change; settle for 60 percent at first.

4. Do not shame or reject your child. Never say, "Shame on you" or "I won't love you." Do not give a 10-minute lecture on every behavior. Use short—the shorter the better—simple words to make your point.

5. Evaluate whether your child acts up after being overstimulated by too much television.

6. Evaluate whether your child is overstimulated by too much activity. Some children need a bridge between hectic activity and quiet time. They benefit by a calming-down time: a bath, being read a story, or *listening* to a record or cassette.

7. Most young children outgrow their frustrating behavior as they learn to speak and articulate what they want. Parents see marked improvement when the child is three years old. If your child remains difficult, talk to your pediatrician.

8. Sometimes children act disagreeable or stubborn when they are becoming ill or recovering.

9. Rather than respond only to your child's negative behavior, try to look for good behavior, and reward it with hugs, kisses, and praise.

10. Let yourself be human. No technique works always, and no parent has patience every second. Do not try to be perfect. Try to be the best person you can be, and the rest will follow.

15

TODDLERS AND CHORES

HURDLE: *Who cleans the mess?*

GOAL: *Secure cooperation and good habits*

Owen J. angrily looked at the jumble of toys cluttering his three-year-old daughter Samantha's room. He had repeatedly ordered her to clean up, yet every toy was on the floor. Since this was not the first time they had clashed over clean-up, Owen decided to teach Samantha a lesson. He gathered her toys, saying, "I told you I wanted you to clean up and you didn't, so now I am going to throw away your toys." In his outrage, his only solution was drastic, because he was so furious he wanted his child to suffer for disobeying him.

Getting toddlers to cooperate and tidy a room seems nearly impossible, yet this is probably one of the most important tasks they learn, one with long-lasting consequences for the family's peace. Clean-up is a bone of contention in many families, especially those who establish their rules too late. With persistence, you can teach young children how to organize a clean-up chore, whipping the disarray into order. Although parents have varying tolerance for clutter, teaching your child to clean up is a valuable, lifelong organizational skill.

Carol J. disagreed with her husband Owen's approach, so they negotiated how to solve the problem and then they launched serious efforts to have Samantha participate in the clean-up. They recognized orders were ineffective because Samantha had no idea of what to do or where to begin. "She cried because she didn't understand and she was overwhelmed." The couple turned to a children's book, *The Berenstain Bears and the Messy Room*, by Stan and Jan Berenstain, which comes as an audio or video cassette that you may be able to borrow from the library.

In this book, all the toys are removed from the messy room until a toy box and shelves are built. Both parents help organize and fix up the room. In the J.'s case, Owen says, "We put the toys in a big plastic bag, and I told her we would hold the toys until she learned to clean up. We *showed* her what we wanted, and we told her that for each day she cleaned up, one toy would be returned."

Once her toys were back, Samantha had learned a valuable lesson. Now the J.'s only have to threaten to get out the plastic bag and remove the toys, and she cleans up promptly. Beside the punishment from her parents, Samantha now understands precisely what their commands mean.

Children must understand the words you use to be able to comply with an order, such as putting away their toys. The first time you use a general command, such as "clean up," someone must show a young child how to proceed and exactly what to do. Children can look like they oppose you, but they are merely bewildered.

Sometimes toddlers have good intentions, even offering to help, but unless an adult guides them through the activity and helps them stick with it, they wander away from the task. Sara T., two and a half, was playing with toy cars in nursery school when the teacher signaled a change of activity on the piano, enthusiastically singing the refrain, "Cleanup 1, 2, 3. I'll help you and you help me." Sara eagerly put one car in the bin, got distracted, and left the rest to the teacher. Sara avoided the chore, not by being deliberately lazy, but by finding some other activity infinitely more interesting.

Here are additional key points to help your toddler learn to cooperate in clean-up chores:

1. Examine your behavior about cleaning up, because children model your actions. Although you may be neat and your spouse messy, your child will not necessarily choose neatness over clutter, so you and your spouse may have to negotiate behavior.

2. Even when your toddler is one year old, begin talking to him about what you are doing as you return the toys to their rightful shelf or toy box. "We are going to clean up *by* putting your toy train back in the toy box." Hold up the train and replace it in the toy box. The key idea here is to help your toddler learn the words that eventually form your commands. He learns by example and by repetition.

3. Avoid yelling or physical punishment to make your point about chores. Force teaches children nothing. Help children understand the task by giving them clear, careful instructions.

4. Break the job into parts. First, tell your youngster you will put away all the books on the floor. A general command to clean up a big mess confuses and terrifies children.

5. When possible, use bookshelves or crates for toys to teach your child a sense of order. If every toy has a little home, clean-up is much easier.

6. Children are notoriously slow, even when they are cooperative. Do not assume the whole burden yourself just to hurry them. You can help, but it is more important that they participate than getting the task done quickly.

7. Shut off the television to avoid any distractions. Keep her mind on the chore.

8. Say, "If you want to color next, then we must clean up now." Introduce the clean up with this phrase, and soon he gets used to the idea of cleaning up after himself.

9. Allowing children to help means giving up some control of the final product. Perhaps the shelves are not quite as neat when children restore their toys, but youngsters gain a great sense of accomplishment if you allow them to do chores independently, without criticism.

10. Praise your child for being neat, for putting the toy back in the right place, and for helping. Do not use words alone. Use hugs and kisses to get your point across.

11. Tell your spouse or another person how helpful the child was when your youngster is within earshot.

12. If you punish your child for not cleaning up and you tell her the consequences are losing a story, do not let her wheedle you out of the consequences. Follow through. She will never obey you if you are a pushover.

13. Make clean-up fun. Sing, play a game like How Fast Can You Return the Toys, or play music. Use an hourglass or timer to set the speed.

14. When guests visit, set aside the last 15 minutes for Helper Chores. Say, "In our family, everyone helps clean up."

15. Like Sara, adults also know that no one likes to clean up, especially alone. Make clean-up time a family workout and do chores with your children. They learn how to do chores from this process, and they get the special feeling of being an active member of the family team.

16. When clean-up is finished and the room is tidy, make sure the child does not miss noticing how terrific it is to have order and calm once again. Besides acknowledging the child's help, say, "Doesn't this room look great? It's so nice to have the toys out of the way, and now we have a place to sit quietly where we can read a story." Or you can say, "Doesn't the table look nice after it is wiped clean?" This gives your child a chance to appreciate the value of cleaning up.

16

DESTRUCTIVE DISCIPLINE AND CONSTRUCTIVE DISCIPLINE

HURDLE: *Letting anger control you*
GOAL: *Learn to be more effective*

Marlene told her three year old to bring his undershirts up to his room four times, yet the undershirts remained on the chair. Believing the child was ignoring her request, Marlene bellowed at him. "I didn't mean to get so angry, but I was furious that he was not listening and I was frustrated."

If you always exert power or if you are constantly in the role of teacher, your child never gets a chance to learn about his individual qualities, elements that distinguish him from everyone else. Encouraging his individuality while making things happen in your home requires considering the difference between constructive and destructive discipline approaches.

Among the negative methods of discipline are yelling and spanking. Although yelling or spanking a child's hand or bottom is successful for shock value if they are rarely used, these methods affect a child's self-esteem, her inner image of herself. Think of self-esteem as a large rubber tire. When you yell or spank, you deflate the tire. Daily yelling and spanking also deflate your child's self-image, not to mention yours. If you consistently lose control and yell, even if you never spank your child, your child learns nothing about cooperation or motivation.

To avoid destructive discipline, consider how life feels for little children—always looking up at a giant, who says lots of words, many of which they do not understand. When you ask a child to bring his shirts upstairs, you may want the task done immediately, but how does your child know this detail? Without being told this piece of information, he thinks he has a choice of when to comply. His choice is do it later, and this unintentionally frustrates you. Distinguish between those tasks you want done quickly and those that can wait. Clearly state your request. You could say, "I want you to bring the undershirts upstairs now, so please stop for a moment and take them. Here they are." Or you could say, "When you finish putting together the puzzle, please bring the undershirts upstairs." Explicit requests take a bit more energy, but they leave no room for doubt about what you want accomplished.

Sometimes parents make polite requests that invite opposition. After reviewing how she gave directions, Marlene realized she often said, "Would you mind doing this?" Or, "Could you do this?" Avoid open-ended questions that lead children to believe they control the answer. Be assertive, explicit, firm, and kind. If you believe the task must be performed quickly, state your directive explicitly, "Put the puzzle away now. Here is the box."

When you are direct, if you must punish the child for not complying, she understands those consequences better.

But do not go around barking orders like an army general. Instead, take your request to another level by enlisting your child's assistance. Toddlers love to have a "job" or to be "helpers." They also perform amazingly well when they believe you think highly of them, especially after you praise their efforts. This positive training helps them learn about follow-through and about completing a project.

Many parents effectively use a timer, and when it goes off, the child must stop and complete the assigned chore. Timers work because they are impersonal, and they help you dodge some nagging. Warning: Use the timer sparingly because you cannot have timer bells dinging all day or they will become ineffective.

If a minor problem, such as spilling milk, becomes a daily battle, instead of scolding your child let him help you mop up the mess. Children who are learning to drink from a cup may topple the cup once a day. If you are responsible for cleaning the puddle each time, your child may take longer to try hard not to spill the milk. Hand him the paper towels: let him help mop it up. When he has some responsibility for clean-up, he starts to concentrate on keeping the cup balanced.

Positive discipline means choosing your battles. Do not make everything into a power struggle. Sometimes parents try too hard to achieve perfect behavior from their children. It is fine to overlook some behavior. If you let some details slide, you may feel relieved, not burdened.

Remember, your feelings may show on your face, although you try to control your voice. Our children are so tuned into our behavior that when one mother merely raised her eyebrows and whispered to rebuke her son, he asked her why she was yelling. In a child's mind, yelling is not volume, but a feeling.

Here are additional key points to help you become more effective as you discipline your child:

1. Use humor, not to tease your child, but to loosen yourself up. Even if you think of something funny without saying it aloud, it can relax you.
2. Do not try to manipulate a child by telling her she hurt your feelings. Tell her you're "disappointed" with her action.
3. If you are irritated over something that has nothing to do with your child, explain to a three or four year old that you are having a bad day. Youngsters can be sensitive to your feelings. One mother who felt like everything went wrong one day exasperatedly asked her crying nine-month-old baby, "Why are you doing this to me?" Her three year old responded, "We love you Mommy."
4. Try to exercise; fitness is as important to our sense of well-being as it is to our children's.
5. Do not talk to other people about your child as though he is invisible. You may inadvertently reinforce poor behavior. Treat him with respect.
6. Do not ask or wait for other people to discipline your child. Children feel safer when their parents take on this responsibility themselves.
7. One way to avoid destructive discipline is to avoid potential conflict by identifying your child's trigger factors and either avoid them or try to figure out a new approach.
8. As parents, you are entitled to make some rules nonnegotiable.
9. If your child has cereal on herself and the floor, if you can't find her last pair of matching socks, if the hamster is loose in your living room, and *you* have a temper tantrum, remember: There is always tomorrow. Nobody's perfect.

17

THE FAMILY NAME

HURDLE: *Our child disgraces us in public*
GOAL: *Learn when to ignore other people's reactions*

At playgroup one day, Edith J.'s son, Max, two, slapped her so hard her head fell back. She ignored him. At the next playgroup, which was in her home, he slapped two children. Embarrassed, Edith tried two time-out periods, which stopped the behavior during playtime. Hours later, however, when they were alone, Max slapped Edith again. "I lost it. I yelled, 'You want to see how it feels?' I smacked his hands and he looked so insulted."

Edith lost control because she had no discipline plan. Edith felt helpless because her time-out solutions at playgroup were an experiment, not a thoughtful maneuver. When time-out seemed to control Max's behavior, she felt good about herself, but when he reverted to slapping, she felt like *less of a parent*. No one enjoys this experience.

At such moments, other people's children seem patient, well-mannered, and angelic, an ideal that exist in our imagination, which is conjured up when we feel bad. We forget that no child always behaves perfectly. When you are embarrassed and you freeze, consider your goal: Do you want the present behavior to last indefinitely, or do you want it stopped? Although you wonder what other people are thinking, do not silently write their script. We are not mind readers. You may believe your in-laws think, "My, isn't he an awful dad" when they really think, "Wow, he's brave to stand up for what he believes." Learn to tolerate feeling uncomfortable, because the payoff is helping the child learn to behave.

Some parents argue that even with a goal, they hate scenes, they dislike showing anger in public, and they want to maintain a calm appearance. Others find anger threatening because they worry that if they let their temper go, even just a tiny bit, they will lose control, beat their child, or act foolishly. Such a feeling is scary. Developing a plan helps these parents rehearse their limits.

Edith, for example, planned her strategy well before the next playgroup meeting. Before leaving that morning, Edith warned Max, "Slapping is not nice, Max, and if you do it, you will miss your playgroup." At playgroup, almost predictably Max slapped her, and Edith responded firmly, "I have warned you about slapping Mommy. Now we will have to leave the playgroup." Apologizing to the other mothers and children, she took the screaming Max home. She patiently reinforced this consequence by firmly repeating, "You may not hit Mommy."

She reinforced the idea by saying each day, "Little boys may not hit mommies." Before, she worried about raising the topic because she thought it would remind Max to hit. Now she had confidence because she knew if he hit, she would provide the consequences. Before leaving for playgroup the next week, Edith reminded him he would miss the fun of playing with the other children if he was naughty. He behaved; now he knew she would follow through with her threat.

When you deal with a young toddler, describe what you want. Make yourself say the words, because we do not know what young children understand, and even if they do not understand at first, through repetition they catch the point eventually.

In a home or a restaurant we can effectively use time-out with a warning and a choice for youngsters who are three and older. We can take the child to the bathroom or the car. Firmly say, "I want to speak to you privately." Once away from the others, speak firmly and softly, but keep your face stern.

One mother took her four year old out of the restaurant and into their car, where she said, "You have two choices: You can sit in your seat in the restaurant and not play with your food and talk loudly, or we leave immediately and miss the fun of being with everyone, and I will not take you to a restaurant for a long time." She paused long enough for the words to settle in and then added, "Now, think it over and tell me your choice." Her threat worked because she had a history of carrying through on consequences.

Here are additional key points to help you handle embarrassment:

1. Evaluate your private behavior with your child. You cannot control children publicly if you do not control them at home.
2. Act decisively in public when your child misbehaves by saying something or by taking the child aside. Do not pretend the incident did not happen.
3. State the consequences of misbehavior clearly, and ask, "Do you want to leave? Do you want a time-out?" Your child gets to choose, but your

ultimate weapon is having him know you will do exactly what you say you will do.

4. Show disapproval. Say, "I don't like the way you are behaving," even if you are in a situation you cannot leave.

5. Do not ignore misbehavior, because if you ignore acting out, later you are likely to explode in frustration and your youngster may not understand what happened.

6. Analyze the situation if your child misbehaved and you did not discipline her. Who was around? How did you feel about your child? About yourself? Rehearse how you would have liked to act, and prepare for the next time by rewriting the script with a new ending to help yourself cope better, with a positive attitude.

7. Sometimes embarrassment leads to worry about what is *normal* behavior, a parent's code word for psychological problems. One way to make yourself feel better is to discuss development with your pediatrician, to learn about normal behavior for children who are your youngster's age.

8. Do not ignore impossible behavior or vacillate between approaches. The inconsistency confuses children, who need direction.

9. When children frequently misbehave in public, it is tempting to try to avoid these situations by leaving the children at home. Many parents, if they can afford it, get babysitters and limit these encounters. In the long run, however, parents and children benefit by being together in public. It is important to teach children that *you* are in control.

10. If behavior in public has become a bone of contention, it sometimes helps to explain clearly

to the child before you leave the house where you are going and how you expect him to behave. Set the ground rules before leaving the door, and outline the consequences for misbehavior. Children need to know what kind of behavior we expect from them.

18

~~~~~~

THE GUEST'S RESPONSIBILITIES

HURDLE: *Our friend does not understand children*

GOAL: *Set behavior standards for company manners*

Alex W. invited his long-time college friend, Brenda F., to visit with her two young sons. As Alex and Brenda talked, the youngsters jumped on Alex's camel-colored, overstuffed suede couches—with their shoes on. Brenda was oblivious. Alex was furious that his friend showed so little respect for his property. The topic of whether your child possesses acceptable company manners is like body odor. No one wants to raise it with their friends or relatives, but many hosts privately report resentment of parents who act indifferently. Children cannot be expected to understand polite standards until their parents provide a blueprint for how to behave in other peoples' homes.

Alex did not tell Brenda he was annoyed. Because she ignored her boys, he was forced into the role of disciplinarian to protect his possessions, which made him angrier. Quickly, Alex invited Brenda and her boys out of the apartment, "willing to buy them lunch, brunch, or dinner, anything to get them out." Since that day he has never invited Brenda back to his apartment. "I never will, either, until those boys are safely away in college," he says.

Passively tolerating certain behavior may be acceptable in your home, but children who do not feel responsible for being nice to others (manners) or for caring for other people's property (respect) ultimately behave in immature, inappropriate, and unappealing ways. Others prefer not to be around children whose parents do not tell them how the world expects them to behave.

Sometimes someone outside the family explains to a lucky child what is unappealing about his behavior. Mitchell G., 11, had a friend he adored, but whenever Tom visited, the entire G. family rebelled and complained about Tom's behavior. Finally Mitchell sat Tom down and said, "You're not exactly the most popular person in my family, and you know why? It is because you act up."

Mitchell gave Tom a structure for his behavior by defining some limits or "family rules" for his friend. He also gave Tom the purpose for the behavior: by acting more calmly, by not climbing on our furniture, by asking permission to go to the refrigerator, people will like you better. After that Sunday, everyone in the G. family happily remarked that Tom had changed.

Parents of young children are often overwhelmed when their toddler misbehaves, so they ignore the youngster's actions. They also feel uncomfortable disciplining the youngster while people watch because they are unsure of what they are doing.

Many parents believe discipline is an all-or-nothing task, and they get angry. Others view discipline as punishment or taking something away. Still other parents dislike making their children unhappy. Dr. Nancy Engel agrees that when a child looks unhappy or cries, those sad or insulted faces "tug at the parent's emotional self."

But Dr. Engel says parents forget they need not summon anger to train their children. They can be kind and gentle and still make their point. They can identify with the child's discomfort and feel some of her distress even while lovingly putting into action a plan of discipline. Children need discipline, she points out, because they feel protected when their parents set limits for them. Limits help children understand how the world is organized and what is expected of them so they can behave maturely and appropriately.

Here are additional key points to help you show your youngster how to be an appealing guest:

1. Although toddlers are typically messy and you cannot prevent mess or spills, you can keep your child at the table, cover the furniture, use a bib, and wipe off sticky hands before the child leaves the table or high chair.
2. Do not let children climb on the furniture, particularly with their shoes on.
3. Be sure that your child says please, thank-you, and you're welcome. When you do not tolerate demands, your child is not demanding with others.
4. Sometimes children act up in another person's home because they want your attention. One father takes his son for walks to break up the monotony of family visits. Other parents provide distractions such as toys, puzzles, or books.
5. By helping your toddler behave as a guest, you help him learn appropriate behavior for the moments he is not with you. You invest in the future.
6. Try to tolerate embarrassment, and do not talk about your child as though she is invisible. Some

parents say—usually with nervous laughter—"Ha, Ha. I can't get her to listen and...." Researchers still do not know enough about children's understanding, but by repeating information, your youngster learns you will not stop her. Instead of talking *about* her, talk directly *to* her. Tell her what you expect. Do not use the word *can't* because it leaves room for discussion. Say, I do not want you to do that, and try to interest her in a new or favorite toy you have taken along.

7. When visiting with very small children, bring along a playpen or stroller and toys.

8. Do not turn a visit into a war between the family members if you or your child is criticized. We become defensive when deep down we feel insecure.

9. Once you initiate a discipline plan that you follow wherever you are, your child learns you are credible. After awhile all you need to do is start to get up, raise your eyebrow, or shake your finger, and he will get the message.

10. At times, even with careful planning, your child misbehaves in public. Review what happened, or discuss it with your spouse to see how you can handle things better the next time.

11. Keep the rules for young children the same at home and in public. Acting differently in public and private confuses children, who stretch the limits of behavior.

19

~~~~~~

REWARDS

HURDLE: *Our child doesn't obey unless we bribe him*

GOAL: *Use rewards effectively*

L ois C. rewards her child each time she does something well, like using the potty and helping clean up. Lois' sister, who is pregnant, wonders whether it is right to reward children for behavior you consider reasonable.

Little children do not come fully equipped with an understanding of reasonable behavior. We help them acquire this knowledge by talking to them and by showing them appropriate behavior. We drive our message home by offering them rewards. How, when, and what we offer as incentives make a difference in our relationship with our child and how our child thinks about his behavior.

The distinction between rewards and bribes is not moral but psychological because it falls into an area of behavior that addresses motivation. Parents reward children to encourage positive behavior. The difference between a reward and a bribe is intent. In the parental arena, bribes substitute for action or affection.

Rewards, the tokens we give freely, need not possess cash value. Rewards are extra attention from parents or smiles, kisses, hugs, praise, or feedback, a verbal explanation.

Feedback is extra information to help children make sense of your actions. Two parents, for example, rode up in a hospital elevator with their twin boys. The father held one boy, while the other one clutched his leg and begged to be picked up. When the father urged the mother to pick up the youngster, she asked the little boy, "Do you want me to pick you up?" The little boy resisted, as would any of us, because the message, perhaps unintended, was that she did not want to pick him up. Besides, she seemed to speak for the benefit of the people in the elevator.

So the child pleaded with his father to pick him up, but his father remained silent. His mother said his father could not pick him up because he was holding his brother. The youngster looked frightened and troubled since neither his mother nor his father explained why he could not be held. He knew his father was holding his brother. He needed feedback, the cherished prize that helps us understand what is happening. Some feedback could include:

"You had a turn just a while ago. Now it's Eric's turn."

"Eric isn't feeling well so daddy is holding him. When he puts him down you will have a turn."

"It's too crowded in this elevator for me to hold both of you. I will pick you up when we get off."

Warning: Feedback will not suddenly change your child into an angel. In the elevator incident, the child might not have liked the feedback, so he might have continued to ask his father to pick him up, but he would have known his parents were sensitive or tuned into him. Rewards do not always "get" children to do something. They reinforce the message that you care about your child. Sometimes silence conveys rejection.

A cherished reward is positive feedback, which strengthens obedience, generosity, or honesty and raises our self-esteem, our inner voice that reminds us that we are delightful people. When someone sincerely thanks us or says, "terrific," we feel good about ourselves. You can raise a child's self-esteem by giving her modest rewards that cost only a bit of time.

Modest rewards help parents avoid trapping the child into a search for the "right" answer. Also, rewards carried to excess discourage a child who inwardly feels intimidated or forced into a behavior. A great big reward raises doubt in a child's mind because excessive praise feels slightly fake. He wonders if he should believe you. Was his behavior *that* good? Does he have to behave even better tomorrow to have you praise him so lavishly?

A modest reward is a lovely way to reinforce moments when the child focuses on the joy of meeting a challenge, learning something hard, learning something new, or remembering what we said yesterday. Rewards are not just words, but a physical connection. While speaking, touch your child, look into her eyes, and then say,

"You worked so hard on that picture and you used such pretty colors."

"That's wonderful. You remembered the sound dogs make."

"Terrific. I'm proud of you for remembering to say please."

Unlike rewards, bribes do not improve our relationships with our children because we offer them when we want quick results and we do not have the energy to explain why. They do not have much to do with the child except that he is an obstacle. Here is one scenario:

Mom: "C'mon, it is time to go to the store."

Child: "I don't want to go to the store. I hate the store."

Mom: "If you go, I'll buy you a lollipop."

If we offer bribes frequently, we risk having the child always expect something in return for her actions. This expectation sets up conditions for conflict because no parent wants to come up with a tangible item every time a child behaves reasonably or cooperates, or every time he or she wants a child to do something.

Here are additional key points to consider about rewards and bribes:

1. Think twice before offering food as a bribe or depriving a child of dessert because you may emphasize food too much, creating a new problem with consequences for your child's weight.

2. Remember that your behavior constitutes your child's first experience with the world. If you are too indulgent with bribes or lavish rewards on him, he will expect rewards and bribes from others, so you set him up for disappointment.

3. Think about your feelings when you think about rewards. What words make us feel good about ourselves?

4. Sometimes a bit of extra consideration or a reward changes a child's behavior. One mother did not want her children to eat the candy she put out for guests, but no matter what she said, they persisted. Finally she hit upon a solution: she gave the children a special plate filled with goodies for them that they could eat in the kitchen for their "party," and the guest's treats were no longer in jeopardy.

5. Reward or feedback that helps youngsters understand positive behavior arises from your reports of what you feel when they behave positively. In their book, *How to Talk So Kids Will Listen & Listen So Kids Will Talk*, Adele Faber and Elaine Mazlish suggest using these phrases:
   It's a pleasure to see...
   I feel happy when...
   I am pleased that...

20

~~~~~~

DISCIPLINE HELPERS WITHOUT RIVALRY

HURDLE: *Trying not to compare brothers and sisters*

GOAL: *Find methods to boost sibling relationships*

Just after bathtime, during a cozy, warm moment, Lily, two and a half, looked up at her older sister Abby, age five. "Abby, you look so big to me. You look just like— (pause)—a mother."

Since younger and older siblings admire each other, parents can successfully use their feelings to inspire youngsters. So much is written about sibling rivalry, jealousy, and displacement we ignore the positive effects of competition, trust, and companionship. We forget how family relationships positively influence children's behavior. Whether our children relate to each other constructively depends on our behavior toward them as a unit and as individuals.

Their relationship expands even when we are not watching, as Larry and Minna Z. learned. They worried about two-year-old Claudia, who never sat still when they tried to read her a book. Their elder daughter had loved books from one year on, and she always sat quietly during reading time. Larry and Minna feared their restless younger child had an attention deficit disorder.

But one day, Minna went into Claudia's room. She picked up a book from the crib. As she removed the book, Claudia announced, *Hello Rock*, which was the title. Surprised, Minna turned the page. With each turn, Claudia "read" the text.

Although Claudia disliked having her parents read to her, she adored having her older sister read to her. Marion, who enjoyed having her parents read to her, passed along the pleasure by imitating them without their knowledge. It seemed that Marion climbed into Claudia's crib each morning with a book.

Such spontaneous, tender relationships between siblings start with permission to experience anger. Larry and Minna had explained to Marion she did not have to "love" her sister and she could even hate her sister. Marion's favorite story was about when Minna's sister was born; her mother admitted hating her little sister because she was a "boring, unwelcome intruder." Although Larry and Minna allowed Marion's angry feelings, they set limits on her angry behavior. Their family rule was firm: she could not hurt her sister, a rule that safely confined Marion's bad feelings. Family rules act like little enclosures for children by helping them understand exactly where the walls of behavior begin and end.

In homes where both siblings feel they have a special place, they positively influence each other. Competition revs up their activity engine. One seven-year-old child refused to learn how to ride a bicycle until his four-year-old brother was minutes away from learning. Then the older boy rode down the street—in time to beat out the younger. The positive side of competition is that it often helps us get ahead.

Parents can't enlist siblings to help each other if they pit the children against each other by making discriminating, insulting comparisons that ensure bitterness. It is unkind to use one child as a standard against which to measure the other child. Don't say, "Janie sits quietly. Why can't you?" Such remarks guarantee sibling resentment.

Remember that early on, little children carefully monitor what you say to them and to their siblings. They also observe your *reactions* to the siblings, and they carefully compare how you react to them. Many current studies establish that little children develop a great interest in other family members' behavior by one year. Children especially tune into emotional exchanges like compliments or scolding, writes Judy Dunn, Professor of Human Development at Pennsylvania State University.

This means you must consider what another child in the room may hear. Dunn wrote about her observations of a 30-month-old child and his 14-month-old sister:

"Andy was a rather timid and sensitive child, cautious, unconfident and compliant. His younger sister, Susie, was a striking contrast—asssertive, determined, and a handful for her mother, who was nevertheless delighted by her boisterous daughter." During an observation of Andy and Susie, the little girl persistently attempted to grab a forbidden object on a high kitchen counter, despite her mother's repeated prohibitions. "Finally, she succeeded and Andy overheard his mother warmly, affectionately comment on Susie's action: 'Susie, you *are* a determined little devil.' Andy, sadly, commented to his mother, '*I'm* not a determined little devil!' His mother replied, laughing, 'No! What are you? A poor old boy!'"

Perhaps this mother was teasing her son, but little children are literal. Since they cannot understand teasing at their expense, they feel sad and rejected, because, as Andy did, the child tries to make sense of the words. He evaluates himself and he may inaccurately believe something is wrong with him. Differences are a strength. When siblings see their separate strong points respected at home, they learn to respect each other's gifts. They also get along better in a diverse world.

In Dunn's example, the mother could have enlisted Andy and bolstered his self-esteem by replying, "No! You are a determined big helper and together we have to watch Susie so she doesn't hurt herself." Or she could simply say, "No! You are a determined big guy." Sensitively monitoring what you say can salvage pride and discourage children from resenting each other.

Here are additional key points to consider as you enlist siblings without rivalry:

1. Do not always try to treat siblings equally: just treat them fairly.
2. Remember, children should not always have to help with siblings. They need time alone, and they need privacy.
3. Acts of fairness, love, and respect encourage kind feelings between siblings, promoting a desire to help each other.
4. Do not worry about siblings who argue. Sibling disputes help children to learn how relationships work and provide valuable lessons about trust and friendship.
5. Treat children as if you have confidence in them: Instead of harming each other, they become responsible and unite for their mutual benefit.

21

HOW WOULD YOU FEEL IF...

HURDLE: *Our child seems insensitive*
GOAL: *Teach children empathy*

Two-year-old children are not "the picture of sensitivity," but as they approach three years, parents report changes in their sensitivity. Margaret S. notices how Andrew adopts her musical sound when he greets his sister after a nap, saying, "Hi, Sweetie." If his sister cries, he stops playing and runs to her, soothing her by saying, "It's okay."

By the time they are four years old, children demonstrate deeper understanding and sensitivity for others. In a discussion about whether children should see "serious" movies, Ellen G., a nursery school teacher, asked three little boys why "little children find some movies scary." A four year old insightfully commented, "Because they think those things can happen to them."

As most children develop, they connect with friends and siblings by sharing, cooperating, helping, and showing unselfish concern because their parents encourage and provide guidelines for this behavior. Teaching children how to behave considerately is part of a discipline plan that includes such ideas as supervising their whereabouts, teaching children to solve problems by themselves, correcting misbehavior and reinforcing desired behavior, and talking with children about our feelings and those of others.

We encourage children to imitate our tone and our words by our amusement and approval, which sends the message that their feelings and behavior are appropriate. When we praise children or tell them they have acted appropriately, they puff up with pride and think well of themselves. When we think well of ourselves, we are said to have good self-esteem.

Besides direct discipline, our children learn by watching us respond to others. When playgroup member Yvette L.'s daughter was hospitalized, Marge S. called her often, asking how the S. family could help. Marge and her husband Len prepared a "care package" for the L.'s. Children absorb values by watching them in action. You know they have absorbed these values by their actions and words. Out of great concern for her mother's feelings, a three year old gently told her mother, "I love you very much, but why don't you stay upstairs by yourself sometimes?" By correctly repeating her mother's script, "I love you very much—but..." she showed she understood.

Parents sometimes worry that by teaching their children to be unselfish, they inhibit the children's competitiveness. Have faith in your child's ability to distinguish between kindness and competition. Consider this example. One father reports his six-year-old daughter came home from school one day and carefully sorted through her school papers, separating them into two piles. He asked her what she was doing. "Sandy is sick and I told the teacher I would bring her work home from school, but I don't want my papers to get mixed in with hers because I don't want her to get ahead of me."

Although children exhibit kindness, they may not recognize an uncaring act until we point it out to them. Four-year-old Karen F. disappeared on the playground, causing her mother great anxiety until she found the child. "I was so angry I wanted to spank her, but I desperately wanted to teach her not to walk away without telling me, so I asked her, 'How would you feel if I walked away from you without telling you?'"

"The question obviously struck a nerve, because after that, she told me where she was going. I realized she understood the idea behind *how would you feel*? Weeks later I tried the sentence on my younger daughter. My mother came for a visit bringing the two girls dolls, one with blonde hair and one with brunette hair. The younger girl, three, angrily claimed she wanted her sister's doll. I asked her to come inside so I could speak to her privately, and I asked, 'How would you feel if you brought someone a toy and they made a great big fuss because they wanted a different one?' Wouldn't you feel bad?"

This child listened intently and returned to her grandmother. "Grandma," she asked hesitantly, "can I see you privately?" The child apologized for the fuss.

Here are additional key points to consider as you help children learn considerate behavior:

1. Children must feel secure and trusting before they can act kindly toward others. They develop security and trust when they have parents who do not lie to them and when their parents protect them. In nursery school a child who offers to help a classmate clean up a spill uses lessons from home. She acts kindly because she has learned it is appropriate, and she is secure, believing in herself.

91

2. Children imitate your language, so avoid making unkind or judgmental comments.

3. Children cannot be ordered to be unselfish or considerate. In one psychological study, researchers ordered children to share their bowling winnings with needy children, which they did. Later, however, their sharing behavior declined sharply and they displayed a greater incidence of stealing, perhaps because they resented the adult pressure or perhaps they felt deprived of their winnings.

4. Children feel unpressured about their behavior if you explain why their actions are important; they need to understand your logic, and this takes time and effort to explain.

5. Children and adults can gain physical benefits from generous behavior. In his book about self-esteem and stress, Allen Mendler, Ph.D. writes that people feel calmer and freer from stress when they help others.

6. Children warm to your approval, a lovely reward for considerate behavior. At first they may need rewards; eventually they act in ways that benefit others without expecting such a reward.

7. Teaching children manners—how to say please, thank-you, and you're welcome—is another way we teach considerate behavior, because when we respect people, we display thoughtfulness.

22

TELEPHONES AND CHILDREN

HURDLE: *Our toddler wants to use the phone*
GOAL: *Learn about early training for the telephone*

While the babysitter diapered his sister, Jake S., 22 months, climbed up on a chair near the table holding the telephone. He looked at the buttons and chose one. He held the receiver to his ear. His friend answered, and Jake invited him over. The friend's mother knew something was wrong when the babysitter answered the door and looked rather surprised to see the neighbor's son and hear Mrs. H. announce, "Here he is."

As young as he was, Jake understood precisely the power of communicating by phone, but he did not understand the limits of his powers. Discipline in terms of the telephone is not punishment but instruction. We teach our children about the telephone and the rules that apply to this instrument to help them learn about respect for other people's time, tolerate waiting for their parents to finish a conversation, respect the diversion, know they have boundaries, and how to handle the phone in emergencies.

It would have been pointless to punish Jake. After all, he used his brain to solve a problem, such as wanting a playmate. You do not want to discourage initiative, but you can explain the rules. Jake's mother explained to him that she wants him to ask children over to the house when she is home, and she wants him to ask permission before taking it upon himself to act.

Many toddlers enjoy answering the phone, but this can annoy some of your friends and relatives. Did you ever try to make a quick phone call, only to reach a youngster and then try to talk your way past a chatty toddler who is under the impression you called for him? Or perhaps you reached a child who answered the phone, said she would get her parent, and promptly forgot. It can be infuriating. Also, people worry that leaving a message with a toddler is like sending the message to a black hole.

The same child who likes to use the phone hates having his parents talk on the phone. Although the child plays quietly alone while you read the newspaper, when you answer the phone, he acts like he is impersonating a foghorn. Children sense you can put down the newspaper, but they know perfectly well how absorbed you become while talking on the phone. This does not mean you should give up using the phone, but when children act up a lot when you are on the phone, question how much time you spend on the telephone.

The telephone, which presents certain dilemmas, can save lives. Not too long ago a story broke on CNN about a four-year-old boy who saved his mother's life after she fell into a diabetic coma. The child related how he tried to open his mother's eyes; when he could not, he ran downstairs for sugar and then dialed 911 to report the emergency. The child was nationally celebrated for being a hero, which he was, but his parents should have been celebrated also. This child knew how to handle this emergency because his parents had talked openly with him, and he knew how to get help because he had been taught how to use the telephone and instructed to memorize the 911 number.

Here are additional key points to consider when you begin early training to teach your toddler about the telephone:

1. Do not leave phone wires around where children can chew on them. These are a safety hazard.
2. If you allow your toddler to answer the telephone, instruct her to say, "Hello, this is... Here's Mommy (or Here's Daddy)." Also instruct her to immediately turn the phone over to you.
3. If your child likes talking on the phone, confine his chatty conversations to mommy, daddy, or grandparents.
4. Since children quickly learn to recognize which buttons on the automatically programmed phone represent various individuals, let them know the rules about making calls. You can let them press the buttons, but they must ask permission to call someone.
5. If children act up when you are on the phone, take a moment from the call to distract them with a toy, explaining you will be finished soon. Then be sensitive to the time.
6. Sometimes events in the family or neighborhood cause you to spend much time on the phone, which you cannot prevent. One man spent hours dealing with hospitals and doctors when his mother had a stroke. Young children cannot understand such a lengthy diversion. The best you can do under these circumstances is acknowledge what happened: "I know I was on the phone so long." Then offer to spend time with your child. "Let's play with the LEGO now and then I will

95

read you a story." You may be exhausted from your ordeal, but that extra 30 to 45 minutes pays off in a calmer, happier child, and instead of feeling defensive and guilty, you feel happier also.

7. If for some reason, after an emotional round of calls, you feel you cannot deal with your child, apologize. "Sweetie, I know this isn't fun. I feel really bad." Hold your child, hug her, and even if she doesn't stop fussing or crying, know that you tried your best. We cannot always make everything all right.

8. Some parents find that holding conversations on a portable phone help children tolerate phone time because parents seem more available. Also, you can walk around and monitor young children.

9. Teach children their phone number—and address—as soon as possible. By four, children should be able to memorize this information.

10. In states where 911 is the emergency number, teach it to your child or teach him to dial 0. Teach children to dial nine-one-one, not nine-eleven. Children may waste valuable time looking for the numeral eleven.

11. If you conduct business from your home, you can tell children three years and older that they absolutely must be quiet when you are on a "business call." Children can understand such rules. One mother has repeated this rule so often that her two-and-a-half-year-old daughter, when playing with her toy phone, says, "Mommy, I'm on a business call."

12. When possible, hold business conversations away from the children. Be sure someone is watching them and they are safe.

13. Do not insist that children talk on the phone. Many callers are too polite to refuse to listen to them, yet it can be annoying. Also, it is tempting to have children show off their verbal skills, but many children will not perform on command. Parents should not get into a power struggle over this issue.

23

~~~~~~

RULES IN THE SUPERMARKET OR THE STORE

HURDLE: *Our child wants to buy everything*

GOAL: *Help our child understand limits*

A three-year-old boy ran along the aisle in a well-known toy store gripping a toy, the price tag flying through the air. When he reached his mother, who was examining games, he breathlessly asked, "Mommy, Mommy, is this toy too 'spensive?" She looked at the price tag and nodded yes. He looked sad, but without an argument he dashed off to replace the toy.

This story is real, not some parent's idea of an idyllic situation. It happened, but only after horrendous scenes in the supermarket when the child was much younger. The scenes were horrendous because the youngster shrieked when his mother refused to buy an item. "Anyone who has experienced this," says Gina H., "would probably never take their child shopping again."

Yet much is to be gained by taking a toddler shopping and enduring their anger in a supermarket or store when you refuse to buy them an item. This is your chance to teach children your particular family rules about buying and, more generally, how to behave in a store. You also begin the lessons of being smart, discriminating consumers and you teach them to delay gratification. When these lessons are learned early, you avoid many dilemmas later.

From Gina's perspective, she says she learned with her other two children the importance of early discipline. When toddlers learn that you resist crying and whining after you say "no" in a store, they behave better. Gina's comments are on target, but in a sense they are misleading because she omitted the rest of the story.

Her children learned this lesson because both parents reinforced it with consistency, with occasional rewards, and with reasonableness and fairness. They followed a set of guidelines, including never take your children shopping just before lunch or dinner.

You can bet that a young child who enters the supermarket just before mealtime wants all the food in sight. Who can blame him? If there is no way out of a shopping trip, carry some healthy snacks, such as raisins, orange juice, or a small piece of cheese, which elevate his blood sugar and help him be less cranky. Avoid giving him sweets because these cause cavities and they raise the blood sugar quickly and then lower it, so he may be charming as you search through the aisles, but when you reach the checkout, he may be howling.

Another guideline to remember is that some children hate shopping. If you take them with you, remember to talk to them and make sure they are comfortable. Make your child comfortable by removing heavy outer clothing when you are indoors. When you drive around in the car, have fun with your child. Sing songs, recite nursery rhymes, and tell stories. One mother's extra time alone in the car with her younger child made shopping an opportunity to inflate her son's self-esteem as she shouted, "Who's the greatest little boy in the world?" She said, "I could practically see his sense of self puffing up right there. Besides, none of his siblings were around so there were no jealousy issues."

Here are lessons derived from shopping trips:

- Shopping reinforces prereading skills. From the time children are two and a half years old, they can identify products from the commercials they see on television. Play the game of finding the product. It's fun.
- Children can learn consumer power when they see you use coupons or make choices based on price. From three years old on, you can explain about saving money.
- Children can learn to make choices and decisions, if you let older toddlers choose between two products.
- Children can learn about eating healthy foods, if you talk about the foods you consider healthy and those you consider unhealthy.
- Children can begin to learn critical thinking skills if you talk to them about truth in advertising. One resource for teaching this is *Free to Be You*, a record by Marlo Thomas.
- Children can learn how to stand up for their rights by your example in the store when you ask a manager to open a new register if there is a long line.
- Children can learn about honest feelings if you feel badly—different from feeling guilty—about not being able to buy them something they want because it costs too much.
- Children can learn the difference between needs and wants.

Here are additional key points to help you make a shopping trip fun:

1. Learn to avoid battles. Distraction is a powerful tool. Offer a restless child a toy that you took along for such a moment, which was safely tucked away in your purse. Play Clap Hands for a moment.

2. Hug and kiss your child while she is quiet during the shopping trip, because to understand disapproval, a youngster must feel your warm approval.

3. Prepare a list so that instead of concentrating solely on shopping, you can at times concentrate on your child and make eye contact; talk to him. Sometimes we are so goal oriented, we forget what a little generous attention can accomplish.

4. When you let your child out of the cart, firmly establish the rule of "no running in the store." Not only can children damage the displays, but they can accidentally knock someone over.

5. Let children "help" you by placing some items in the cart.

6. Reinforce positive behavior in stores. Children dislike shopping, and they act up so they can leave a boring store. If you must shop with your child, bring along a book or toy. Some positive attention helps make the experience better. Tell your child you appreciate her patience, you know this is taking long, but it will be over soon.

7. Remove children's hats and coats indoors in the winter because they can get overheated. Consider their physical comfort.

24

WHEN FRIENDS'
PARENTS HAVE
DIFFERENT RULES

HURDLE: *Our friends let the children go wild*
GOAL: *Help our child learn about differences*

Pizza flew across the table, and the children spit, howled, and fought. "Dinner was a mess," sighs Myra E., remembering the night she and her daughter Caitlin, three, had dinner with a neighbor and her two sons, four and six. "One child grabbed a paper crown and declared himself king, and his older brother then threw a temper tantrum, screaming, "It's not fair." Myra wished the hostess parent would stop the chaos. Instead, the mother sympathetically asked her quarrelsome child, "Did you have a hard day?"

Myra had a hard time understanding why this mother dealt with feelings instead of the immediate problem. "When we get beyond the basics, we try to interpret children's behavior, and we make mistakes."

Parents often silently disagree with the methods neighbors and relatives use to discipline their children. Such disagreements become sensitive when friends have very different rules and your child wants to try the other family's rules at home.

Children naturally bring home new and different behaviors. Parents say that before they took their child visiting or let him play with the children next door, they were happy with their child's behavior. "Then, suddenly, our child's behavior seems polluted," says Aaron Zuckerberg, M.D., a Baltimore pediatrician and the father of two children. "Then parents must turn to the task of helping their child learn to discriminate between behaviors."

You can change *your* child's behavior, but you cannot change relatives' and friends' behavior. Not permitting your child to play with these other children solves nothing because we can never avoid (and neither can our children) all the people who are potentially bad influences. The best defense is learning how to resist such influences, and the best time to learn is when children are young.

Myra's and her neighbor's distinct styles of disciplining forecast a clash. Myra's friend views discipline as "understanding" children and "validating" their feelings. "She is more permissive, and she deals with emotions and feelings and analyzes their behavior for deeper meaning," says Myra. Myra's critique reflects her and her husband's preferences. Both view discipline as "shaping" behavior, a method, Myra says, that considers children's feelings but actively defines parental expectations.

Whatever our philosophy, we are predictably irritated when youngsters arrive home with new and unwanted behaviors, words, or phrases. Fran N.'s daughter Louise, four, quickly recognized that her playmate manipulated her parents by throwing a temper tantrum, so Louise came home and threw a tantrum when she wanted a new toy. Trying out new behaviors or new words are ways children work to form their distinctive personalities. Louise tried on a new behavior just as someone tries on a new hat.

At first Fran did not understand why her sunny child was acting so terribly until Louise bluntly said, "Annie's mommy gives her whatever she wants when she cries." Aha! Fran sat on the floor next to Louise and explained, "Different mommies have different ways of doing things. I love you very much, but sometimes mommies have to tell their little girls they can't have a new toy." Louise accepted the difference in rules.

Talking about family rules gives a structure to your views. It's like drawing a picture of a house and finishing it off with a neat little fence around the garden, the house and the backyard. When youngsters know they have family rules around them, they feel safe. A family rule indicates the family has values, beliefs they will defend or sacrifice to preserve.

Often firmer action is needed in addition to words. When young Gregory came home and jumped on the couch because Eddie's mother let him do this in her house, Gregory's mother did not tell him not to jump on the couch because the couch cost so much money. Even if she had received the couch free, she would be careful with her couch. Gregory's mother told him the family rule is to treat property carefully.

Here are additional key points to consider when dealing with families who have rules that differ from yours:

1. Regard misbehavior as an opportunity, not a catastrophe. The opportunity now exists for you to explain that there are differences between families.
2. Keep explanations short and simple. Remember the KISS principle: Keep It Simple Sweetie.
3. Avoid sounding as if one rule is better than another: it is simply different.

4. Discipline is a long-range plan, and you want your child to incorporate your values when he is young. Later, when you are not around, you know he still follows the family rule.

5. You help teach your children your rules so that you can eventually trust them. When you feel ready to give up, think of how many families do not trust their teenagers. Act as though you believe your child will do the right thing and follow instructions. With practice or experience, continuous explanations, and reinforcement, children learn to recognize and react to friends who try to influence them negatively by not following those friends.

6. Try to avoid letting a new behavior continue so long that you work yourself into a screaming frazzle and then try to explain what your child did wrong and how she "forced" you into this outburst. Instead, be assertive. Assertive parents firmly say two sentences uttered one at a time in this order: "I'm telling you to...." Speak firmly and keep your face stern although you may waver. Children need to believe you are in control. If the child does nothing, then say, "Last chance. Either you do this or I will...." Explain the consequences of not acting.

7. Recognize that parents should not act cruelly to children in the name of family discipline or family rules. In a recent *New York Times* article about tennis parents, a Florida father said he whipped his children with a stick to create "respect" for him. Hurting a child is abuse. If you cannot control your child without extreme measures, then something is wrong and you need to address the problem.

25

APOLOGIZING TO OUR CHILD

HURDLE: *Not knowing when to back down*
GOAL: *Discriminate between respect and weakness*

When Michael O. asked his mom for a cookie, Rose remembers automatically saying "no." "Then he started to whine, and I went to battle." Halfway through saying "no" for the third time, she suddenly asked herself why she was arguing. Silently she wondered why it mattered whether he had a cookie.

We want to apologize when we realize we have entered a routine power struggle, trapping ourselves in an unwanted battle. Parents feel unsure about apologizing, however, because they think an apology signals weakness. They wonder, who is the boss? Being the boss is not the issue: being fair is the issue. Children learn to trust a parent who is free of bias.

There is a canyon of difference between losing gracefully and weakness. Regularly changing your mind or apologizing may signal weakness. If, despite apologies, you continue to see negative behavior, you may need to step in with discipline. Consider the critical questions:

1. Do I want a child who...?
2. In my heart, what do I consider important?

When your child misbehaves and you punish him by taking away storytime, he may try his darndest to wheedle you out of the punishment. After a disagreement, a child wonders where he stands with his parents.

To understand this feeling, think of arguments with your spouse. When someone is angry with us, we want assurances of love. Little children, learning about the limits of anger, may think anger means abandonment, withdrawal of love, or even withdrawal of support. Parents help children overcome such fears when they separate the child's behavior from her as a person. Tell your child you love her, *but you do not love what she did.*

"Sometimes I know we fight over something stupid, but I can't find a graceful way out," says Rose. It feels this way to Rose, yet she has taught her son an important skill. Michael, at two years and four months, is quite verbal. He negotiates whenever she says "no." When he asked to get some grapes from the new refrigerator, which is easy for him to open, Rose warned him not to take any. In lawyerly fashion, Michael pleaded his case: "Just one grape, mommy. I won't make a mess. I'll be careful." Amused, Rose softened, increasing Michael's appreciation for bargaining and his understanding that he can state his case.

Bargaining helps parents and children save face. Problems over negotiations arise because Michael and other young children do not understand their limits. Although we may yield a point when children present a logical, rational argument, we also have the right to decide which behavior issues are nonnegotiable. We do not bargain over physical safety, for example.

Sometimes parents realize they overreacted or wrongly blamed the child. An apology shows respect for your child and teaches him that in a loving family people make

107

mistakes, are forgiven, and are loved. Kay G. "owns up to her shortcomings," because, she says, "it's easier to say you're sorry and go ahead from there rather than being defensive about your guilt, which will be more time consuming."

Young children may hold a grudge. Bernie D. says, "We say we're sorry, but David doesn't want to hear it. When *he* says 'sorry,' the incident is over. When *we* say we're sorry, he's still angry." Adults who receive an apology can switch emotional gears much faster than little children, who need time to advance from anger to happiness. Give your young child time to think it over, and try to approach her again. If she refuses, wait; she will come around.

An apology can acknowledge our child's feelings, a wonderfully freeing gift for a young child who feels confusion and anger simultaneously. When David's mom gave birth to his baby sister, he stayed with his aunt that day, but he was lonely and confused. When his father arrived, David was so angry, he called Bernie "a bad daddy."

Bernie sensitively said, "I'm sorry you think I am a bad daddy. Are you angry that I left you with Aunt Lorna?" When the child nodded, Bernie said, "Dad's back now." Bernie reports the youngster understood and he seemed to calm down. "He fell asleep next to me, and then I put him in his bed." Bernie's apology was compassionate, simple, clean, and direct. It did the trick without frills.

Parents apologize easier than children, who do not always understand why you want them to apologize. Encourage children to own up to their shortcomings, but do not stand over them and demand that they apologize, or they learn about losing through force and control, not about expressing regret. Your anger does not help them experience the feeling of regret.

One father says his two-year-old son becomes "stubborn" when asked to apologize. "Rather than say he's sorry, he hides in a corner." Two year olds have much to learn about apologies; three year olds can say they are sorry, but parents must help them understand how to change behavior. By four, children say they are sorry, and they understand you expect them to avoid certain behaviors.

Here are additional key points to consider about backing away from a decision and apologizing:

1. Children must learn that apologies are not automatic excuses for misbehavior. Saying you are sorry does not allow you to continue to act rudely.

2. Children must learn when an apology is a routine expression of regret (accidentally bumping into someone) and when it signals our intention to change our behavior, a subtle lesson that takes time to teach.

3. Children watch and listen to us handle our errors, and by observation, they learn mistakes are not disasters. If we acknowledge our mistakes, forgive ourselves, and change, we teach them to forgive themselves and change behavior.

4. Children must accept responsibility for wrongdoing, something we do when we admit an error.

5. Just saying you are sorry is sometimes not enough, and the family needs to discuss what happened. Discussions air the issue and help avoid pointless arguments in the future. Discussions can lead to a friendlier conclusion.

6. At times, accept an apology as a sign of good faith instead of angrily asking, "Why did you? How could you?" Often people cannot explain an action, but they are grateful for a second chance.

26

~~~~~~

ANSWERING BACK

HURDLE: *Our child wants the last word*

GOAL: *Find techniques to settle disputes*

In the middle of a snowy afternoon, Lauren, four and a half, was bored. Since her mother also suffered cabin fever, she bent two rules. First, she permitted Lauren to make chocolate milk by herself. Lauren carefully poured the milk and slowly added the syrup to a cup without a top. Ordinarily she drank from a cup with a top. Today seemed special indeed because two rules were bent. Then, Lauren said she wanted a straw. Her mother replied, "You did a great job making the chocolate milk, but if you put a straw in that cup without a top, it will tip." Lauren answered back, "No, I want a straw." She marched directly to the cabinet, retrieved a straw, and put it in the milk. Her angry mother poured the milk down the sink.

Four year olds like to assert their power, but having a small child assert herself by saying "no" in a loud voice is like waving a red flag in front of a bull. In this incident, Lauren challenged her mother because she saw the rules changing in front of her, so she wondered whether a third rule could be broken. Her mother needed to clearly state, "No. I do not want you to get a straw. Either drink the milk without the straw or we will spill it out. What is your choice?" Once the warning was delivered, she needed to reinforce her words by standing up and stopping her child from reaching the cabinet. Words and body language let children know you mean business.

If you do not appear firm, children translate your polite approach as indecision, and when they believe you may give way, they press ahead with what they want. In doing so, they may cross the boundaries of appropriate behavior. If you let this pass without addressing what is happening, they learn nothing about appropriate behavior. When toddlers behave rudely and they are not called on it, they continue to behave this way as older children and then as teenagers—and it becomes decidedly unattractive.

Listen to your oppositional two year old, and imagine trying to control him as a teenager spewing insults at you. Jason R.'s dad believed in reasoning with his son when the boy misbehaved, but their long discussions typically ended with verbal explosions and four-year-old Jason screaming at his father, "I don't like you. Get out of my face." Imagine Jason R. at 14 bullying his father, and you visualize the difficulties of reining in a rude adolescent.

Of course, not every angry verbal outburst represents a problem. Children have a right to their angry feelings, and we need not feel like monsters if our child says "I hate you," nor should we worry about occasional sassy statements. Children may just tell it like it is. When Cary R.'s daughter said "I hate you," Cary responded by saying, "I understand. Sometimes I hate what you are doing, but I always love you." Cary's breezy attitude and her words helped her child observe an adult response to angry words. Cary validated her daughter's feelings and reconfirmed her love, providing a safe haven for her youngster.

Sibling rivalry can produce verbal outbursts, as Betsy L. discovered when she brought her tiny son home. Her three-year-old daughter angrily said, "You have a new baby. I want a new mommy." Betsy pretended to leave the house; when her daughter cried, she returned and hugged her little girl. She made her point: "You will always be my Sally, and I will always be your mommy."

When children carry their conduct and words beyond reasonable limits, we must help them understand that when we value people, we do not speak to them in ways that hurt them. They also must learn that sometimes they must accept no as the final answer.

When Dawn M.'s grandmother tried to discipline her, Dawn disrespectfully called her grandmother "a wicked witch." The first time Dawn did this, her parents thought it amusing. Yet after three times, the remark was not funny, but still Dawn's parents did not reprimand her. Although her attempts to rein in Dawn were met with silence from her daughter and son-in-law, Dawn's grandmother said nothing because she lived with Dawn's family. She felt uncomfortable about reprimanding her granddaughter or being critical of the child's parents.

So Dawn controlled this family, hating every moment of her power. Like other children who wield power, she exercised it outwardly as a little dictator, but inwardly Dawn was insecure and frightened. She feared a counter-attack since power makes little children feel insecure and it makes them worry that they will be punished, yet they cannot and will not stop themselves without adult help.

Here are additional key points to consider when you hear your child answer back:

1. Do not follow every inconsiderate remark with disciplinary action. Sometimes just enjoy a child's spunk or his creative way with words.

2. Many children who have behavioral problems in school have not learned to exercise impulse control over their words. Parents need to help children learn when remarks are appropriate and when they are not.

3. Reflect about how you or your spouse verbally treat others, because your child may imitate your words and tone.

4. Do not tolerate rude, hurtful remarks. Take children three years or older aside. Hold them as you explain that you expect them to stop these remarks. Holding conveys the key idea that setting rules and love are equivalent ideas.

5. If you see a situation developing that clearly has the potential for negative behavior, you have a responsibility to stop it before it becomes a full-blown battle. Clearly state what you expect in words.

6. Share your reasons for disliking fresh answers so your child eventually understands the logic behind your commands. Children respond well to explanations. For them, it is like being let in on a secret, and it is rewarding to see their eyes light up with understanding.

7. Sometimes children, like adults, answer back because they are cranky, irritable, or ill. Once parents rule out illness, then they should talk to the child and explain the ground rules of behavior. Children will not understand what you expect unless you clearly state your demands. Even after clearly stating what you expect, you may have to take further disciplinary action. One father commented that his three-year-old daughter spoke rudely just after she awakened in the morning. He found that by asking her to take a time-out "until

she could apologize and speak to me properly" allowed her the opportunity to decide to change her approach. Another mother commented that time-out would not work for her son, and she had to have long discussions at a time when she was in a rush. "It was worth it. Sometimes you have to take the time even when you do not think you have the time."

27

DAWDLING AND FORGETFULNESS

HURDLE: *How can we end infuriating habits?*
GOAL: *Teach memory and organizational skills*

In one week Samantha G., four, lost her spring jacket, her T-shirt, and her eyeglasses. Her parents, Philip and Betty G., were furious. They wanted to know the ideal punishment for Samantha to quickly "teach" her to take care of her belongings.

Two houses down the street, Mike H., three, dawdles. He dresses slowly in the morning, or if his parents tell him to fetch his jacket, he starts for the closet, gets distracted, and forgets they are waiting. Because he is little, most mornings his mother tolerates his dallying, yet when they must leave on time, his behavior irritates and infuriates her. When they have a deadline, she dresses him.

Dawdling and forgetfulness are two maddening behaviors that parents overlook in young children, yet these signal troubling habits. Dawdling slowly blooms into procrastination, and forgetting signals inattention. Instead of waiting for these tendencies to worsen, help your young children master time management and organizational abilities.

Children dawdle for two key reasons, says Renee Siegel, a former nursery school teacher. "Either they want

115

attention or they are daydreaming. The little girl who breaks her snack into 10 pieces and is still nibbling that snack when everyone else has dashed off to get a book for storytime wants her teacher to sit with her and give her attention by urging her to finish."

Children forget their belongings because they are not focused, says Siegel, but parents can help them develop concentration and keep their attention centered. Developing attention in young children begins with small family routines that we take for granted, such as explicitly expecting your child to come to the table at the same time for meals. "It also means gathering for the meal, not being handed a sandwich to eat on the run," says Siegel. Such routines help your child to start thinking about time and place: these are the roots of organization.

Children learn tidiness from simple tasks, such as taking off a jacket, mittens, and hat. "Parents can teach them to do this in an orderly way," says Siegel. Talk to your child as you proceed; explain what you are doing. Say, "First, we take off your coat; then we take off your mittens and we put your mittens in your jacket pocket so you will find them easily when you need them."

Youngsters also learn organizational skills as they watch you and help you clean up. They learn about the idea that each item has its place, and they learn to appreciate neatness. Living in an uncluttered environment provides people with feelings of control over their lives.

Like forgetfulness, dawdling can also be prevented. Notice whether your child dawdles because he wants the extra attention. If this is the case, begin giving him extra attention in a more positive manner by playing with him. Put puzzles together, build towers, read storybooks, or go for an adventure on the bus, subway, or train.

Some children, particularly creative children, are quite the little daydreamers. The key is not to stop a child from daydreaming but to help her learn when it is important to attend to the assignment at hand.

Sometimes these children need advance warning about a change in pace or by telling them an activity needs careful attention. To alert them about a change in pace, explain the activity sequence. Say, "You can play with this for awhile, then you are going to take a bath." Explaining a progression of events helps prepare children to switch gears.

Transitions are hard for children who dislike changing activities. Here, consistency helps. Children find life confusing, for example when you let them remain in their pajamas for five mornings and on the sixth morning you expect them to dress quickly. Early in their lives, set expectations for performance, such as dressing and being ready on time. Stick to your system.

Here are additional key points to remember as you try to avoid the habits of forgetting and dawdling:

1. Discipline for these habits does not mean figuring out an appropriate punishment. It means teaching your child to concentrate.
2. Whenever you talk to your child and explain either an activity or what you expect, be careful not to swamp him with words. Keep it simple.
3. Organize your home so toys and clothes have a place. You do not have to be superorganized. Toys, for example, can be piled in a toy box, not methodically on shelves.
4. Although your child may be quite verbal, little children do not understand sophisticated concepts like the "value of money." If they forget a

toy somewhere or lose one, talking about the dollar value of the item does not impress young children.

5. When something is lost, emphasize how to change behavior by explaining how your child can avoid this next time. Explain, for example, that taking her boots and putting them together in the cubby at nursery school helps reduce the possibility of loss. Make your child understand she must concentrate on her behavior.

6. Do not lecture or preach. Make your point, and drop it.

7. Allow mistakes. When children or adults are excited or overloaded by entering a new or different situation—like the first week at school—they can forget where they put items. Just think about how often you may have misplaced your keys.

8. Give your child an incentive to move faster by rewarding him with a hug or a kiss, or make a game of getting ready by beating a timer or racing Daddy.

9. When you make exceptions to the rule of eating at the table or getting dressed by eight in the morning, explain your reasons and make it clear the exception is for today only.

10. If your child dawdles or is forgetful, set goals for improved behavior. Select a plan, and stick to it. If you drop the plan, you may lose the struggle. Discipline is changing the child's behavior and yours. Do not expect immediate improvement, but expect progress.

28

BRINGING FRIENDS
HOME

HURDLE: *How can we encourage children to play here?*
GOAL: *Learn social give and take*

When Alice M. started nursery school at age four, the M.'s collectively heaved a huge sigh of relief. "It was so hard for her to separate from us that when she happily went to nursery school, it was like a huge burden fell from us," says her dad, Dan. "But now we faced a new hurdle: We wanted Alice to experience friendship."

The M.'s recognized that parents provide the building blocks of social skills: practice, experience, self-esteem, and the ability to separate from parents. Friendship is an important social skill, because having friends is an important component of life.

Children need not be social butterflies to be healthy. "Having friends is a matter of degree and preference," says David Forbes, a Harvard psychologist, who researches child friendships. Forbes points out that youngsters who connect to others are "much more likely to be able to adapt to life's tragic events, such as the loss of loved ones."

At first, young children engage in fantasy play with their playmates, which helps them learn about how people are supposed to get along in social situations. It gives them practice at cooperating and at thinking about their actions and other children's actions. Even in early childhood, says Forbes, children accumulate information about how people get along.

Parents help their children make friends from the first time they sign up their children for a playgroup or invite another youngster over to play. Dan M. asked the nursery school teacher for a list of Alice's classmates, and he and his wife systematically called the youngsters one at a time and arranged for them to play with Alice.

Since the M.'s took the initiative, the first playmate arrived at their home and Alice played on her turf. Playing on home turf is not as important for a child with good social skills, but a child who has difficulty separating sometimes feels more comfortable playing on home turf. Within the safety of her home, she can learn the rules of social give and take, and being at home sometimes gives her more confidence.

Children can learn much about cooperation, reasoning, and judgment in the roles of both hosts and guests. Hosts are called upon to share toys. Guests learn to ask permission to play with a host's toys. Guests also learn about the host family's rules for activities.

These early experiences permit children to feel competent about relating to people outside their homes. In turn, a feeling of competence enhances your child's self-esteem, an important element of friendship. What seems to make the difference between social success and failure is the child's self-esteem, his inner opinion of himself.

When a child has a positive inner opinion, it sounds like the little voice in *The Little Engine that Could*, a child's storybook. The inner voice tells children, "I think I can, I think I can." Competent children believe they can take care of themselves physically, and manage home and school problems, and they believe their ideas, opinions, and decisions count.

The child to be concerned about is the child who is always isolated, who no one ever picks for a friend, or the child who is a scapegoat, says Robert Selman, a Massachusetts psychologist who has researched child friendships.

Selman defines the stages of child friendship roughly by age, although there is overlap because of individual differences. Between two and five, children choose friends on a casual basis because of physical attributes, who has the best toys, or proximity. Between four and eight, children treat friendship as a one-way relationship. They think nothing of rejecting a friend, nor do they think of the impact of their actions. At these ages, children do not view friendship as a continuous commitment.

Somewhere between 5 and 14, children begin to be influenced by friends enough to worry about rejection. But, says Selman, they still do not choose friends based on values. After 12, they understand that getting to know a peer is a step-by-step process, but they do not reach the highest stage—sharing and intimacy—until 16 and sometimes not until adulthood.

Here are additional key points to consider as you help children develop social skills:

1. By helping your child enter situations where she can make friends, you help her practice what it is like to give and take in social situations, and you help her get the necessary experience to develop social skills that promote friendship.

2. Avoid overscheduling children's social lives. Children need time to relax and to play quietly, and they need quiet time near you. Try to strike a balance among your time, quiet time, and time with friends.

3. Try to limit playovers that extend through dinnertime. Eating at a friend's house once in awhile is great fun, but if your young child is eating at someone else's home more than twice a week, review his schedule. Such engagements create a long, exhausting, and often overstimulating day for children.

4. Beware of pressuring your child to succeed socially. In the book *Children Under Pressure*, Helen Heffernan writes that young children search for acceptance one way or another because acceptance is a basic human need. Parents should help children, she says, find positive types of peer acceptance. "Keeping up with the crowd is really a sign of immaturity, but one has to live a long time to discover it."

5. Parents need to show children how they treat their friends, how they make new friends, and how they deal with problem situations. When parents have close friends and relatives, they find their parental effectiveness strengthened by the support.

6. When parents feel good about themselves, they are more likely to help their children be better friends. Children develop the notion of competence partly from parents' love and respect, which translates as feelings of being special, unique, and lovable.

7. Love is not enough. Parents must also provide their children with enough experience to reinforce a belief in competence.

8. Respecting children's opinions extends to their choice of friends. Do not force your child to be friends with another child. Also, try to avoid overstressing social adjustment or having friends. Allow your child to follow her interests and express her individuality.

29

MANNERS

HURDLE: *Our child demands but never says thank-you*

GOAL: *Introduce please and thank-you*

One of two-year-old Michael R.'s first words was thank-you since his parents used the words and phrases please, thank-you, you're welcome, and excuse me. "So we assumed he had good manners," says his dad, David, "but now he's getting sloppy so we have to reinforce his manners by asking him to say please."

Teaching our children manners illustrates one useful piece of parental wisdom. Just when we happily lean back thinking we have taught our children how to do or say something, they seem to forget our message and we need to begin again. Children only remember information with repetition, so if we do not keep up with the repetition, we can lose our struggle to achieve a particular goal. Learning manners represents consideration toward parents, teachers, friends, and relatives, who appreciate politeness and respond to it with kindness and warmth. They find our children likable.

Manners as a topic covers a broad range from saying please and thank-you to such concepts as learning not to touch a birthday cake before it's cut, passing food to someone at the table, taking the piece of food you touch, or asking permission.

Teaching a child manners is a form of discipline that does not depend on what you do to the child but on how well you engage his cooperation. In their book *How to Talk So Kids Will Listen & Listen So Kids Will Talk*, Adele Faber and Elaine Mazlish identify a five-point technique for engaging a child's cooperation:

1. Describe the behavior you see.
2. Give information.
3. Say it with a word.
4. Talk about your feelings.
5. Write a note (remember this item for the future).

Here's how this technique would work to help you teach your child manners. Instead of saying, "How often do I have to tell you not to touch every cookie on the plate?" *Describe* the behavior you want in short, concise terms: Take the first cookie you touch. *Give information* by explaining that children, even when they wash, can have germs on their hand. Taking the first cookie we touch helps us not spread germs. Do not emphasize the germs; emphasize consideration. Remind children about this behavior before they touch the food. Use one word as a reminder: Cookies. Talk about your *feelings*: I don't like it when you touch every cookie on the plate.

Faber and Mazlish stress clearly stating your expectations, which works well with older children. "I expect you not to touch every cookie on the plate."

Between two and two and a half, children can learn to say please, thank-you, and you're welcome. Two year olds begin demanding "me want," and we can gently instruct them to say the polite words, but it may take months for them to perform, depending upon their verbal ability. At two-year-old Michael's home, his dad says, "When we ask him to say please, we engage in a tug of war, holding the toy or item until he says please and thank-you. We ask him to say the 'magic word.' If he doesn't remember the magic word, we won't give him the item."

Just saying please and thank-you does not mean your two-year-old child understands the concept of politeness.

Between three and three and a half, children can learn to follow more subtle rules, such as remaining at the table, not touching all the food on the plate, and asking for permission. They also understand how their behavior is related to consequences, such as approval. They know that if they behave nicely, we are pleased; if they misbehave, we punish them; if they try hard, they learn something new.

Manners, such as not interrupting when a guest is present, are important. Advance planning is the preferred approach. It is unfair to expect polite behavior without help. Prepare for visitors by getting out your child's toys to distract her, inviting over a playmate for her, or perhaps arranging her nap during this period. Planning is playing the game fairly.

You may explain, "Mommy wants to talk with Aunt Bea for a long time, and if you play quietly while we are talking and don't interrupt us, then we will go to the park where you can play on the swings." Rewards give children the incentive to behave, but be fair to your child and try to limit long visits that exclude him.

Here are additional key points to remember when you introduce the topic of manners to your youngster:

1. Children learn manners and respect by watching how we treat others. Do we thank the storekeeper who picked up the glove we dropped? Do we thank our child? Do we say please, thank-you, and you're welcome? Do we ask for directions in a

store by going over to a salesperson and saying, "Excuse me?" Our manners reflect our values, the way we feel about behavior toward others.

2. Teaching manners also helps our children to develop an inner voice that helps them learn impulse control.

3. Help children learn to talk without interrupting everyone else. In his book *Your Child's Health*, pediatrician Barton Schmitt points out that although parents "like children to talk, children need to wait their turn if someone else is talking." Schmitt suggests telling your child that you "will be glad to talk to him when you are finished talking with the other person. Suggest he do something else for now..."

4. Be prepared to follow your requests with consequences if your child disobeys. With children three and older, you can use one warning and then time-out for infractions.

5. Children need to learn that family members are also important, and they need to learn not to interrupt adults during phone calls. Besides setting a clear rule, help your child follow the rule by distracting her with toys or by keeping a box of special toys near the phone, ready for such moments.

6. Be fair, too. Tell your child that if he has something urgent he can say, "Dad, I need you." Long telephone conversations seem to invite interruptions. Try to make calls during naptime or after bedtime, and limit the amount of time you spend on the phone when your child is awake.

30

‸‸

FOOD PREFERENCES

HURDLE: *We make two dinners a night*
GOAL: *Arbitrate food preferences*

D anny N.'s aunt offered him some of her home-baked artichoke pie. Danny, three, a finicky eater, walked over and strolled around the circular table intently inspecting the pie. He squinted at the pie. Then he leaned over and smelled the pie, and that clinched it. "I don't want any," he firmly announced.

Many youngsters decide food preferences based on smell and texture. Unless a parent was a picky eater, he or she may find this attitude toward food annoying.

New research illustrates that parents must evaluate eating behavior within the mysterious confines of genetically determined tastes and appetites. Linda Bartoshuk, Professor at Yale University School of Medicine, says researchers have uncovered three groups of tasters: non-tasters, medium tasters, and supertasters. Supertasters experience some foods as much more bitter or more sweet than other tasters, so many children and adults say Mexican food "burns," milk tastes "sour," and canned vegetables taste "funny," says Bartoshuk.

Even within the confines of genetically determined tastes, parents can set early goals for eating behavior and to encourage healthy habits. Initially parents must bring the spoon to a baby's mouth, but once a child learns food is on the spoon, pediatrician Barton Schmitt, M.D., author of *Your Child's Health*, suggests allowing young children "to initiate the feeding by reaching or leaning forward. Food should not be placed in a child's mouth just because it is inadvertently open."

A one year old's appetite drops sharply. When parents see such a huge change, they worry their child will not get the necessary food requirements. Some feeding struggles also occur now because between one and five, children can go for three or four months without weight gain. Little children's appetites are unpredictable during this time because they grow slowly and need less food. Experts agree no healthy child voluntarily starves himself at this age, but to accurately assess how much or how little a toddler eats, note the variety and amount of food he takes over a whole week. With these facts, discuss his appetite with your pediatrician.

Do not panic if your child refuses a meal. After a no-food meal, your child will probably eat better, particularly if you do not relent and give her a larger snack than is customary. When she refuses a meal, do not quickly offer her an alternative or you may find she expects a separate meal. If you can avoid offering alternatives, she may outgrow some pickiness.

By four or five, says Penelope Leach in her book *Your Growing Child*, children begin to eat more adventurously. "This is a highly imitative stage so eating in company—both at school and at home—often leads children into trying items and dishes they have previously rejected."

Today's nutrition-conscious parents want to help their children choose healthy foods. Here are additional key points to help children develop healthy habits and to prevent them from being too finicky:

1. From the beginning, do not force children to eat. Do not force them to eat every item on the plate. Parents would never dream of hovering over guests and ordering them to eat. Respect your children the same way. Try to make mealtime pleasant.

2. Children who have plenty of exercise generally have healthier appetites. Kenneth Cooper, M.D., M.P.H., author of *Kid Fitness*, believes active children are hungry children.

3. Cooper advises parents to use "visual" techniques to demonstrate why you believe certain foods are not healthy. He suggests that to show children how much sugar is in a 12-ounce glass of cola, scoop out nine teaspoons of sugar and place these in a drinking glass. You, too, will probably stop drinking cola after this demonstration.

4. Do not limit your children to the kinds of foods you like. Try to expand your repertoire, and prepare foods you don't particularly like, such as broccoli or spinach, and let your children decide for themselves. They may like these vegetables.

5. Many children love fast-food hamburgers and french fries, but try to limit the number of meals they eat at these establishments. Explain why you set a limit.

6. Many parents withhold sweets to bribe their children into eating meat and vegetables, an approach that research shows makes the sweets the desired food. The combination of the need to eat forbidden foods with exposure to TV commercials promoting candy and sugar-coated cereals may be why children load up on needless calories that promote cavities.

7. Talk to children four years and older about TV commercials. In the record *Free to Be You*, Marlo Thomas explains that the people on commercials all smile because they are getting paid. Tell young children that commercials do not represent facts.

8. Keep healthy snacks available, including fresh fruit and raw vegetables. By limiting how much sugar children consume, you may reduce cavities and improve their appetites.

9. Many experts report that children who help in the kitchen by peeling vegetables or washing fruit eat better. This is also fun.

10. Try to avoid unnecessary battles. Do not cook something again right away that was recently refused, or you may set up a situation in which children dictate and manipulate you.

11. Many parents have found that when you introduce vegetables before fruits, infants tend to eat the vegetables better. Start with yellow vegetables, then add green vegetables and last, fruit. Also introduce one food at a time, and wait to see if they have an allergic reaction, such as a rash.

12. If for any reason you impose dietary restrictions on children, remember that by age four or five, they may resent these restrictions because it sets them apart from their peers. You can offset such resentment by explaining to your children why you believe these dietary restrictions are important. When you appeal to children's logic, they can tolerate a great deal.

13. Do not give small children peanuts, hot dogs, or lollipops; they can choke easily on these foods.

14. Get CPR (cardiopulmonary resuscitation) training so that if your child chokes, you will know what to do.

31

~~~~~~

SHARING

HURDLE: *Can we get our children to share?*

GOAL: *Discover when sharing is appropriate*

I n Betty R.'s playroom, five 23-month-old children wandered aimlessly, picking up different toys, playing near each other, not together. Over the next six months, the toddlers' ability to talk increased and they socialized more, but they appear more concerned about what toys the other child held than playing together.

Sharing behavior appears when children are three years old. Children must learn to share their toys and their personal space, like backyards (if they have one) or bedrooms; they must learn to share their parents' time with brothers and sisters, and they must learn to cooperate with family members and share family responsibilities. Sharing can present a dilemma for parents and for children because, in terms of time, parents sometimes feel they cannot divide themselves enough. Often parents feel tremendous guilt when they have a second child, because it always seems as though they instruct their older child to wait. Judy L. says that just as she picks up her baby Sara, her son, Michael, three, wants to be held. "I'm constantly saying 'not now,' so my view is that he doesn't share my time. It seems as though he always loses."

This is Judy's perception. Yet in the next breath she adds, "Then I *have to* find the time for Michael later. I look for him, I remind him that I asked him to wait, and then I say, 'Here I am.'" Her guilt made her forget how wonderfully she handled this situation. Often we are too hard on ourselves. Judy forgot she was sensitive to Michael's waiting. Sometimes we remember only how bad we felt about turning down our youngster's request.

Yet learning to wait while we attend to a sibling or sharing time with a sibling has merits. It helps children learn that sharing sometimes means delaying satisfaction, one way we prepare a child to "wait his turn" in school.

The child also learns to cooperate with us agreeably when we explain why she has to wait, if we are fair and remember to give the child her measure of attention and love. She learns to trust our request to wait, and by remembering her, we tell the child that she, too, is a valuable and worthwhile person. This message puffs up her self-esteem, the way she thinks about herself.

We also show the child, by our actions, what fairness means so that he learns to deliver even-handed treatment himself.

Children readily share their possessions with their sisters, brothers, and friends if you show consideration for your child's belongings. When 15-month-old Joshua grabbed his sister's toy, Julie R. said, "If you don't want him to touch your favorite things, put them up higher." She taught Elise a coping strategy, and she confirmed that it was all right to protect her belongings.

Julie also helped her daughter learn how to distract the baby with another toy, and she found a way to allow the older sister to play privately without intrusion. Such a show of consideration conveys love and protection to your child. Children who feel loved and protected can share.

When friends are over, you can help motivate your children to share with these key ideas:

- Children should not have to share everything they own. Take one or two favorite toys and tell your child clearly, "Todd is coming over and I know you'll let him play with your toys. Do you want to put Binky and your favorite truck in the closet (or high on a shelf)? You do not have to share those toys if you don't want to."
- Children should decide what they want to share. Allow your child to select the toys she does not want to share. Limit her selection to two or three favorite items.
- Parents can help by explaining the house rules. If the other child spots the protected toys high on the shelf and asks for them, simply say, "You can play with these other toys. Come look here, have you seen how this fire engine works?" If the discussion persists, simply point out that Mike is sharing all his other toys, but those toys are not for playing. Then turn away and end the talk.

Besides learning how to share their toys, young children can also learn to share family responsibilities. We encourage our children to help by praising their efforts. When a child picks up a toy or puts one away, we respond with smiles, hugs, and words of approval. Then our toddler helps enthusiastically, and feels good about herself as a helper.

Here are additional key points to consider when you want to help your child share:

1. Children need to learn how to decide when to share and how much they want to share. They may feel guilty about wanting to withhold a favorite toy.

2. Learning when and how to share helps a child to be competent, which makes him feel good about himself.

3. Games, such as playing ball, help children learn cooperation. Play ball with your child and a neighbor's child. You will have fun, your child will learn to take a turn, and she will learn to root for the other children, an element of good sports conduct.

4. Watch family television shows with your child, and casually point out examples of sharing and cooperation. Besides using the TV set as a teaching tool, family activities build closeness and warmth.

5. In some families in which children have their own rooms, youngsters may not want to share their friends with their siblings. Many parents support their child's right to ask a brother or sister to remain out of his room during a playover. Siblings who are left out should have time with their parents, or they should have a friend playing with them.

32

DISCIPLINE DURING AND AFTER ILLNESS

HURDLE: *We think we spoil our child when he's sick*
GOAL: *Reinstate the routine*

When Barbara T. was nine months old, her parents celebrated because they "got rid" of her pacifier. They had worked hard to wean the pacifier from their baby daughter. Their merrymaking was short-lived: two weeks later, Barbara ran a 102° fever. "We immediately gave her back her pacifier," recalls Lynn, her mother.

Karen H. had strict rules about television watching and about sitting on the living room couch. Her children watched TV only at certain times in the finished basement, not sitting in the living room on the new velvet couch. Yet, when Karen's son Jeffrey, three, had the mumps, she shelved all rules.

Parents drop discipline when children are ill, and rightfully so. A child who is achy, feverish and flushed needs loving attention. As the child's health improves, however, parents experience new concerns: Have we spoiled our child? Can we get back our old routine without problems?

Children who are sick and cranky display many symptoms that spoiled children exhibit. Barton Schmitt,

M.D. wrote in an article that appeared in *Contemporary Pediatrics* that by age two or three, a "spoiled child" exhibits many of the following behaviors:

- Doesn't follow rules or cooperate with suggestions
- Doesn't respond to No, Stop, or other commands
- Protests everything
- Doesn't know the difference between his needs and his wants
- Insists on having her way
- Makes unfair or excessive demands on others
- Doesn't respect other people's rights
- Tries to control other people
- Has a low frustration tolerance
- Frequently whines or throws tantrums

Cranky behavior that is due to illness is not long-lasting. When children are sick, parents can set aside discipline and focus on making the child feel better. It makes a sick child feel considerably better when he knows some rules are bent in his favor. If he gets a special privilege of watching television all day while sitting on the living room couch as Jeffrey got to do, it helps a bit. As one mother put it, "When I had the flu and a temperature of 102°, I kept wishing my mother would show up with a bowl of chicken soup. Everyone wants to get special care when they are sick."

With children older than three, once the fever or distressing symptoms disappear, you can restore routine fairly quickly by explaining that because they were sick, they got to do some special things. With children under three, it takes patience and repetition because explanations do not mean much to them.

Discipline problems after your child is well can arise for two reasons:

137

1. Your child likes this special treatment.
2. You are still quite anxious, and you have a hard time setting limits.

If your child refuses to settle in and seems to crave the special treatment she got when she was sick, then reevaluate your behavior. Listen to her message. If she got much attention when she was sick, and she seems to miss that bonus, try to build some positive attention into your routine to make her feel good about getting well.

The real problem may not be instituting the routine but overcoming your anxiety, particularly if your child was severely ill or underwent surgery. You may still worry that your child is susceptible to medical or developmental problems, although the medical evidence says he is well. Your hidden fear communicates itself to your child, and it may make him feel vulnerable. Without meaning to, you broadcast the message that he is susceptible to being hurt, that he is still not quite healthy. Also, illness prompts children to become sensitive to their bodily symptoms. When children feel they are not healthy, they doubt their skills and abilities, a major reason that parents who harbor a sense of vulnerability about their children report more behavioral problems with these youngsters, especially in peer relationships and self-control.

No parent can stop worrying. Every parent can think about what messages are being communicated, and every parent can learn to pretend without an acting course. Children cannot read your minds, so when you smile and encourage their independence and efforts after an illness, do so enthusiastically. You may feel fearful inside, but you need not believe your words—you just have to act as though the words are true. This effort inspires enthusiasm in your child, helps her believe she is healthy, and helps her overcome her self-doubts.

Here are additional key points to consider as a child recovers from illness or is getting ill:

1. Be flexible during a child's illness, and do not expect to stick to a routine.

2. Once your child becomes well, point out all the things he can do now that he is better, like go outside, have friends come over, and return to school.

3. If you have a special situation, reach out. Talk to your pediatrician about parent resources, and help yourself by getting involved with other parents who face the same difficulties. One mother and father developed friendships with parents whose children had cerebral palsy. She says, "We became like family. We all made it through together."

4. Sometimes we consider behavior the problem when a cranky child is actually ill. Question whether your child's behavior is a departure from the usual.

5. It is important not to let children think the only time you are nice is when they are sick. Sometimes a parent stays home from work to tend a sick child, and the child—and the parent—enjoy this respite because they rediscover each other. Also, talk to your child about your feelings. Tell him that you enjoyed being with him, and promise the fun will continue. Back the promise by planning a special outing for the weekend.

33

~~~~~~

PRIVACY IN THE HOUSE

HURDLE: *Our family discussions go public*
GOAL: *Learn to speak carefully*

Fran R. recalls an embarrassing moment during her early teaching career. One morning at class Show and Tell, a first grader got up and said he had something to tell. "My mommy got out of the shower and she had a towel around her and my daddy said, 'Drop that towel.'"

Parents sometimes talk freely in front of little children, believing they do not understand. This may be true, but little children often remember word for word their parent's sentences, and they do not always choose appropriate times to repeat what they have heard. Parents cannot punish young children for repeating conversations, but parents can speak carefully around children. Consider the impact of your words as you talk to other adults about your youngsters, and as you discipline and describe your expectations to your youngsters.

Remember that young children are quite literal. They believe what they overhear as fact, says Julie O'Malley, Ph.D., and this can lead to misunderstandings. Because they believe your words as facts, they may hear the information in ways you never intended. One spouse, in the heat of a passing argument may threaten to leave the other spouse. Their child believes his parents are getting divorced.

Since children worry about what they hear, they may repeat the story to friends and relatives or teachers. They repeat the story to try to make sense of the situation, to figure out our intentions, and to figure out what will happen to them. Sometimes they may not repeat what they heard, but they still worry.

Occasionally it takes months for our words to surface, and then the child may repeat our explanations verbatim. Usually we do not mind if information is repeated, but it takes us by surprise. Ruth S., for example, worked hard to have her daughters accept their adoption as a natural part of their lives. One afternoon a new neighbor moved across the street, and Ruth's older daughter went over. She immediately announced, "My name is Tina. I'm four years old and I'm adopted." She happily passed on the information that comprised her identity. Ruth was amused later when she learned about her daughter's statement.

In the course of an ordinary day, as you discipline your child, try to stop and think about possible misunderstandings because your child is literal. In her book *Children's Minds* , Margaret Donaldson includes an anecdote about a young girl disillusioned by her first day of school. She told her mother she waited and waited for "the present" but none was forthcoming. Her mother said she was sure no present was offered. The child reported heatedly, "They did! They said, 'You're Laurie Lee, aren't you? Well just you sit there for the present.' I sat there all day but I never got it." Of course, Laurie Lee did not want to return to school.

Here are additional key points to remember when you communicate to, and around, your children:

1. One aspect of conversation that can confuse young children is overhearing snatches of talk. If a family emergency arises necessitating many phone calls and you cannot make the calls away from your children, try to explain as much as you feel they understand in simple, short sentences. Explanations are necessary because as humans we like stories with a beginning, middle, and end. When we hear only one part of a story, we tend to fill in the rest of the information in our imaginations. Most of the time, what a child imagines is far worse than the truth.

2. Sometimes we try to spare children and unwittingly add to their fears. One mother remembers hearing that her friend's father died by listening to adult conversation. She heard the words *funeral* and *coffin*, but she had never been to a funeral and she did not understand what a coffin is. Her imagination conjured up fearful images that resulted in nightmares for weeks.

3. Not all information should be shared with children. Children do not need to know every detail because they can be burdened unnecessarily. If you decide to withhold information, just talk about it when children are securely out of earshot.

4. Obviously, we cannot watch every word we say. We cannot, nor should we, create a contrived environment for children. Yet we can become sensitive to our youngsters' naïveté, so that we make our disciplinary descriptions, explanations, and commands clearer.

5. We should not punish children when they repeat things because they do not realize they are doing something wrong. You can begin to define the word *private* for children past three.

34

AGGRESSIVE OR
PASSIVE

HURDLE: *Having a child who hits or is a victim*
GOAL: *Teach our child when and when not to fight*

When Amy C. was two and a half years old, she was terrified by the two boys next door. "They were domineering children who would scare her and she'd scream in fear," recalls her mother Elizabeth. Watching your child be physically tormented by another child is a lesson in aggravation for parents who want their children to behave but also want them to defend themselves.

Life is hardly better for the parents of an aggressive toddler who pulls hair or bites other children. "Most of my friends believed that my two-year-old Scott would end up in reform school," said Melissa B. "If another child did not answer him when he said 'hi,' he became angry and bit him."

Whether our child is aggressive or passive, parents try to influence behavior, sometimes overreacting, because we worry that a two year old's behavior represents his behavior at 30. These traits do not define toddlers or slightly older children: children undergo many changes as they grow.

Some aggression or passivity changes as children develop social competence. With gentle guidance, parents can keep a child's behavior within reasonable limits, teaching him either to defend himself or to control his anger. Rather than be angry with neighbors or their children when fights occur between youngsters, help your children think of alternatives to solve the problem.

Amy's parents gave her tools to help her consider alternatives. "We told her if the boys were too wild and they kicked and hurt her, she could leave and go home. We also instructed her to ignore them, not to react every time they seemed to threaten her, because her ready reaction made them taunt her more." Believing Amy needed other children to play with, Elizabeth and her husband Leon enrolled Amy in nursery school, where she could have varied friendship experiences under supervision.

These other experiences helped Amy. Now when she is angry, she can best others. Now she asks the boys next door about their intentions: "Are you going to be wild?" The boys know they will lose their playmate if they are too wild, and they have changed their behavior toward her.

Her parents helped her manage a predicament rather than run away from the bullying youngsters. Helping a child solve a difficult problem produces feelings of competence and confidence.

The parents of an aggressive child also feel helpless, wondering whether they should concentrate on what they believe is correct behavior, not the effects of their discipline.

Donna M. envied her sister, Rebecca J., because she had a well-behaved daughter who was one year older than her son Todd. "I kept saying I wished I had a kid like that." Unlike her sister's daughter, Donna's son Todd, two, was "aggressive, a wanderer, and terribly curious." Donna watched Rebecca forcefully discipline her daughter, order the child to share, and warn her youngster that if she hit, she would be punished. By four years old, Rebecca's child was *too* passive. She had learned her lesson too well.

When Donna saw the effect of being overbearing, she changed her discipline tactics. "Now I let him deal with angry feelings. He normally will not hit back, but he asserts 'No,' and he runs away with the toy. He will not let anyone take advantage of him. He screams at the child, 'No, don't do that to me. I will hit you if you hit me.'"

Donna now reacts positively to his active traits, such as curiosity. When he touches or tries to explore something he should not, she distracts him. She joined a playgroup with Todd to give him group experience in a setting where the teachers would not accept aggressive behavior, reinforcing her lessons at home. The teachers stress "using your words, not your hands."

Here are additional key points to consider when you deal with either an aggressive or a passive child:

1. Psychologists find a connection between regular spankings and increased child aggression. Frequent reasoning and little spanking, these experts note, do not encourage aggression.
2. The children of parents who use more reasoning than spanking seem more acceptable to peers and more cooperative because they know how to negotiate better, and they learn to communicate better. They argue and attack less.
3. Some aggressive children require greater structure to keep out of trouble. These children need to keep a schedule: you need to keep them busy.

4. All children, whether aggressive or passive, need positive reinforcement to help them successfully alter their behavior, including verbal and physical praise, hugs, pats, and smiles. Enlist everyone in the family to provide this reinforcement.

5. Friends can be excellent resources for information. One mother spoke to a friend whose child was also aggressive and passed along her pediatrician's advice: "She said to ignore the hitting child and devote attention to the victim so that the aggressor receives no reward—positive or negative—for his behavior." The mother found this advice helpful, and it worked, she reports.

6. Do not accept a child's immediate and ready apology if you have consistently warned her about hitting. Some children recognize that quickly saying "I'm sorry" is a convenient way to maneuver adults out of delivering consequences. Children should learn that apologies without behavioral changes are meaningless.

7. A "time-out" with an isolation period for the child who is being aggressive can help change behavior if you discuss the issue with the child.

8. Television viewing can overstimulate children, who then become aggressive.

9. Sometimes a "no negotiation" stance works with children who are victims. Mike N., three, was taking a beating from his friends. At first, his parents told him to tell the child's mother, but this produced a bad case of tattling. Then his dad suggested telling the aggressor that hitting hurts, because they may not realize it. This tactic failed. Finally the N.'s said unequivocally, "You *must* hit back." Recently Mike and his mom went to

the park to meet a friend whose son had been tormenting Mike, now four years old. As soon as they arrived, the child immediately grabbed Mike, threw him in the sand and kicked him. Mike got up, squared off, and decked the youngster. Proudly he turned around and said, "Ma, I defended myself!"

35

~~~~~~

WATCHING TELEVISION

HURDLE: *Not knowing what is too much television*
GOAL: *Learn to manage TV viewing*

Four-year-old Nina T. seemed uninterested in television, which seemed curious to her mother, Kate. Kate even worried that Nina might have an eye problem, so she consulted an opthamologist: no problem. Still Nina avoided TV and Kate concluded the child had good taste. One afternoon Nina asked Kate how the television worked. Kate explained about television signals and how programs travel over the wires to our living rooms. Two weeks later, Nina casually remarked, "When I was little, I used to think the people were inside the TV and if it broke, the people could get out."

Television, like a puzzle, is a giant challenge for young children. Like Nina, they struggle to understand how the images appear on the screen, and they try to understand what the images mean. Because children want to understand the world, TV offers parents a discipline opportunity that goes beyond merely managing the amount of time your youngster watches television.

For young children, watching television "is the opposite of the 'empty mind' syndrome," says Daniel Anderson, Ph.D., Professor of Developmental Psychology at the University of Massachusetts at Amherst. Anderson has researched the impact of television on children for more than a decade. "Adults use television for stress relief to replace anxiety—provoking thoughts because they understand the information, but young children find the information novel, a fascinating window on the outside world. They absorb social, even occupational, information that may have long-term implications." Even young children may appear mesmerized by television, but they are absorbing information and thinking hard about what they see, says Anderson.

Some people believe the effect of *too much* television can prompt "the mean world syndrome," a phrase generated by George Gerbner, Dean Emeritus of the Annenberg School of Communications at the University of Pennsylvania. A steady diet of television, he says, promotes the sense that violence solves many problems and generates feelings of insecurity and danger in viewers who identify as potential victims.

Even parents find television hypnotic. Diane L. says she recognizes that as an adult she can be drawn into TV watching so deeply that she has "trouble getting away from it." She and her husband limit TV for their daughter, nearly 3 years old, and their son, 15 months. "I learned that it is easy to get them to settle down by watching TV, and on occasion when they are tough to handle, I use television. We let them watch certain videos they like as a treat, a reward. Our daughter watches one hour in the morning and one-half hour in the evening; then the TV goes off."

By the age of 15, most youngsters spend more hours in front of the television than in school. "They will have spent more hours on only one other activity—sleeping," calculates William Dietz, M.D., Ph.D., Assistant Director of Pediatrics, Tufts University, Boston, speaking at an American Academy of Pediatrics science writers' meeting.

Because such exposure must have an effect, parents should not be embarrassed about regulating children's television viewing. Anderson says, "Parents are not embarrassed to regulate anything else that can potentially have important impact on children, and they prevent children from reading pornographic books or books with needless violence. They should carefully monitor programs that can teach their children objectionable material or that include objectionable content."

Here are some key points to consider as you plan your approach to television viewing:

1. Little children do not know their limits, and they cannot decide for themselves when enough is enough. You must help them by setting limits for television watching.

2. Use your judgment when you read about new research on television watching. Many researchers have a hidden bias, and some use unscientific methods. Television reporters may announce a trend based on research that, with careful reading, does not justify the claim.

3. The American Academy of Pediatrics strongly advises parents not to buy interactive toys. Many of these toys have a "potential to promote violent and aggressive behavior, increase the intellectual passivity with which children view television, and inhibit imaginative play."

4. Parents have a responsibility to watch every TV program and to know the contents of the shows their children watch.

5. Parents can use TV to develop children's critical thinking and enhance their judgment by pointing out how commercials try to sell people toys and other items. They can explain what is true and

what is not true. Even when a TV character makes a bad decision, parents can use the moment to talk about ways to solve problems.

6. Be sure to turn off the television for long periods of time. Many families keep it droning in the background for hours and hours, and voices become part of the environment. You will be surprised at how peaceful and comforting a quiet room feels without an accompanying background hum.

7. Among the activities parents can pursue with little children instead of watching TV are reading library storybooks or planning an art project. Young children love to glue, paint, or play with Play Doh. "Having children sit to develop an art project helps when I am tired," says Dina L., a former teacher. "You can casually monitor them rather than being totally involved. I put my son in a high chair with the artwork on the tray so he can't move around. We use markers, watercolors, cookie cutters, or a toy to cut or make an impression on the Play Doh, different coloring books, crayons, pencils, and pens. We have some painting books that you just brush with water, and the color emerges. I give him a tiny bit of water just enough to clean out brushes, so if it spills it won't make a big mess."

8. One youngster, impressed by a Berenstain book about no-television days, suggested that his family shut off the TV on odd days. "It works well," reports his mother. "On the days we can watch TV, we still limit the programs. My husband and I also follow the no-TV rule. On those days, we read and talk more."

36

HOW TO MANAGE
WHEN WE ARE
EXHAUSTED

HURDLE: *We may make mistakes at the end of the day*
GOAL: *Set a time-out for parents*

Just at four or five o'clock, when a person's temperature slightly rises, Bob S. felt the stress of an exhausting day. Bob and his wife Gail, a physician, now divide their duties so that Bob remains home with the children. This day his older son was acting cranky, the car broke down, and the toilet backed up. Bob was tired, and he still had to plan dinner and finish some cleaning. He felt overwhelmed. For a few moments the house was peaceful as the children, two and four, played safely in the fenced yard. Grateful for the quiet, Bob tried to concentrate on his menu since "cooking is a new thing for me, and it doesn't come naturally."

Suddenly the telephone rang; the children ran inside shrieking. "They had stepped in dog droppings and were tracking them inside the house. The last thing I wanted to do was start mopping the floor and cleaning their shoes." He dived at the children, yelling, "What are you doing?" He scrambled to remove their sneakers and sit them down to avoid their "stepping in it again." Out came the bucket of water and detergent. After cleaning the hardwood floor and their sneakers, Bob felt little like making an appetizing meal.

Every parent can identify with this scene. When we are exhausted, small accidents seem overwhelming. Sometimes children *are* uncontrollable because they too are exhausted. There is no magic energy pill, no exact scientific approach for such moments, but parents can use strategies to lighten these moments.

One tactic is to realize that when we are tired, we sharply feel the lack of personal accomplishment that comes from receiving so little feedback from little children. Psychologists find, for example, that workers who receive frequent positive feedback work for more hours without fatigue than workers who do not receive feedback. Without feedback, parents can temporarily lose motivation and morale.

Besides feeling unappreciated, we also feel unsure, especially with a first child. If you yell at your child when you are exhausted, you can feel anxious, worthless, and sad.

Instead of turning on themselves, parents need to consider exhaustion as an opportunity to teach children about our own boundaries, says Jonathan Reusser, M.S.W, a family therapist who practices in Lexington, Massachusetts. Reusser suggests:

- Consider your needs. "When you are exhausted, you may need to ask children to care for you by asking them not to make demands. Sometimes we need to ask directly."
- Recognize you cannot always give stellar performances as parents, so take responsibility for your exhaustion by saying clearly "I can't help you now" or "not yet."

- Choose your battles. Ask yourself whether their behavior that moment will matter in 10 years. Ask yourself, Do I really want to take a stand here?

People feel better when they believe they can control a situation instead of feeling helpless. One way to feel strong is to view exhaustion as a challenge, not a threat. People who see a challenge adopt coping strategies. Besides, feeling threatened makes us feel helpless, and this can arouse a foreboding sense of deprivation. Feeling challenged can arouse feelings of competence and a capacity to adjust to the situation.

Fred and Dina L. use "team play" when they are exhausted. "Whoever seems more tired and less patient," says Fred, "lets the other parent pick up the slack." The L.'s have two children, a daughter nearly 3 years old and a son 16 months. Fred adds, "We also try to choreograph naps so everyone—mom, dad, and the kids—gets one at the same time. Sometimes it works, sometimes not. We try to get outdoors because cabin fever magnifies the problem. We try to tire them out by going to the park, planning activities, and keeping them busy because then they are easier to manage. Plus, when we have fun together, the day goes faster."

Here are additional key points that parents have found useful:

1. Avoid using the phone when you sense that both you and your child are fatigued. Taking your attention away from a tired child can precipitate a scene.
2. If you shut off the television because you sense the noise is increasing the feelings of strain, consider playing soft, soothing music.

3. Plan ahead. The end of the day is taxing, but some organizational strategy helps. Cook meals in advance. Make several meals at a time and freeze some. Instead of spending the end of the day in a frenzy of housekeeping chores, spend it with your children.

4. Parents need to think about getting to bed early. People deprived of sleep suffer lessened judgment and an inability to feel in control.

5. Stay-at-home parents find Mondays difficult because they split duty on the weekend. Try to help yourself plan an easier Monday to soften the feeling of being abandoned.

6. Experts also suggest using humor. "Humor and your physical well-being are linked," says Dr. William Fry, Associate Clinical Professor Emeritus in the Psychiatry Department at Stanford University. "Laughter has value similar to respiratory therapy. It brings oxygen into the lungs and carries it through the blood. Humor and mirth activate the brain, producing greater alertness and mental vitality. You are more relaxed after a good laugh."

7. Decide what is truly important to you. Do not try to be the perfect parent, housekeeper, or employee. Decide if you can live with less than a perfectly neat house so that you can spend more stress-free time with your children.

37

~~~~~~

WHO'S RIGHT—WE OR THE EXPERTS?

HURDLE: *Swaying with the expert winds*
GOAL: *Understand demands and depend on instincts*

Every family has self-styled "experts." Sue Ellen S. says that during a recent family visit, her husband's aunt suggested that a good child-rearing practice was to "let the child do what he wants, and when he gets hurt, he'll learn he can't do it." Sue Ellen and her husband Rob strongly disagreed, but they kept silent because they did not want to start a family quarrel.

A few weeks later, Sue Ellen told her mother that she and Rob were leaving Kevin in prekindergarten an extra year. "Kevin won't be five until December 30, so he's almost a year younger than the rest of the incoming class." Sue Ellen's mother strongly denounced the decision, insisting her grandson was "very smart." Explaining the decision had nothing to do with his IQ, Sue Ellen said, "We, and his teacher, agree Kevin is smart but he needs time to mature."

Sue Ellen firmly told her mother she and her husband believed in their decision. "We'll do what we think is best." She knew she was introducing a new concept, and she needed to address her mother's fear, that remaining in prekindergarten was not being "left back," an old-fashioned, negative concept.

Most people do not immediately agree with a new idea. Bear in mind that sometimes their first reaction is merely an initial response to a surprise. Arguing is useless, but we can quietly assert our logic for making a decision, and we can remain firm.

Self-styled experts do not make our lives difficult. We do, by reacting intensely out of our desire to "do the right thing," and the prevailing view that there is one perfect model of parenting. Like other myths, this is untrue, but its existence makes us feel defensive.

Educator Joseph Procaccini, coauthor of the book *Parent Burnout*, quoted in a *U.S. News & World Report* article, said, "Some parents 'crucialize'—that is, they have a tendency to turn something that should be routine into something that is critical." Such parents panic over whether they have the right kind of car seat out of insecurity and a belief that there is one perfect answer.

Grandparents and relatives are only one kind of expert. Parents also deal with teachers and doctors who have special skills and knowledge. Their perspective and ours sometimes conflict. You walk a fine balance between knowing your child quite well, and needing to listen.

Meg G. went to visit her son Mike's kindergarten teacher in October of his first year in school. Because Mike was a well-behaved, intelligent youngster, Meg expected praise for her child, but the teacher told her that Mike was overactive, talkative, and generally unpleasant. Shocked, Meg tried to defend her son. She left the school furious with the teacher. By January, Meg was scheduled for another visit; this time she decided not to be defensive. "I just figured if I had a problem, I should give up fighting it and face it." Instead of reacting negatively and becoming the teacher's adversary, she engaged the teacher in a cooperative effort for her son.

In another instance, June K.'s daughter could not get off the couch because every time she did, she vomited or got dizzy. When June took her to the pediatrician, he started with the psychological, "Did the child want to avoid school?" Because June had just moved to the area, she considered that her daughter might have a psychological problem. After thinking it through, however, she explained to the pediatrician that the child had no history of pretending illness. The pediatrician listened and he asked her many different questions. The examination turned up an inner ear infection. June had acted as her child's advocate, something every child needs.

As adults, we need to learn when to listen and when to press for different answers. Here are additional key points to remember when you are weighing expert advice:

1. In terms of your family, you are the key expert. Since we cannot raise children in a vacuum, we need additional information, which we get from experts, such as physicians, teachers, or psychologists, who have specialized knowledge and a larger frame of reference for how families behave. Without this frame of reference, we can distort our beliefs.
2. If you believe an expert reaches an incorrect conclusion, try to explore the logic, how and why the conclusion was reached. Some experts will give you a hard time if you question them, but do not give up. If you are dissatisfied, seek other opinions.
3. Do not worry about "looking good." When we worry about image, we act in ways that handicap

us. We focus on ourselves, not the problem. If you want to ask questions, ask them without worrying whether you look stupid. We cannot be well-informed about every subject, and we learn by asking.

4. Do not hold yourself to an ideal image of parenting. You do not have to be Supermom or Superdad. If you let go of this image, you can weigh what experts say and decide whether you can use the information.

5. Generally grandparents, when they are not overbearing, help quite a bit. Many immigrants or people who move far from relatives have a difficult time, especially with the first child, because they do not have immediate access to the basic information grandparents provide. Do not hesitate to ask questions of relatives; at the same time, do not be afraid to tell them you may not follow their advice, but you want information.

6. When you disagree with grandparents or relatives, make sure you are not automatically disagreeing, but disagreeing with reason.

38

WHEN TO SEEK
OUTSIDE ADVICE

HURDLE: *How do we know if we have a problem?*

GOAL: *Develop a checklist to evaluate difficulties*

A llen S. remembers he and his wife were eager to become parents, but when their son, "who never slept," was five months old, he was hard-pressed to recall "why we wanted him."

Dina L. remembers feeling "so lost" when she had her first child. "I kept wondering, am I doing this right? Even the simplest things some people thought of to solve a problem never occurred to me."

Like other parents today, these parents wanted to solve their troublesome dilemmas but they did not know where to turn. Besides knowing when and how to get help, parents need to separate problems that can be ignored from those needing attention. Inexperienced parents find they distort discipline predicaments, making them bigger or smaller, because they hold two different views simultaneously:

1. They want a solution.
2. They want to ignore the problem, hoping it will disappear.

160

This conflict makes it hard for us to choose a discipline plan, because we ask why we should bother expending energy to develop goals for a problem that will soon disappear. The answer is that some problems do not disappear: they get worse.

Parents resist seeking help because they believe the myth that parenting is a natural instinct. If they need help, they wonder what is wrong, or they believe asking for help is a sign of weakness, says Ann Adalest-Estrin, a child and family therapist and Director of the Parent Resource Association, Wyncote, Pennsylvania.

Today, many parents face discipline dilemmas by linking up with one another in groups across the country to exchange advice, information, and knowledge of services. Parent support groups are one answer for men and women struggling in unfamiliar territory.

Besides knowledge, such groups give parents the confidence that, in another era, parents and grandparents might have provided during the struggle to figure out whether a child's tantrums occur because we are unsatisfactory parents or because the child is testing.

Carla D. took her dilemma about her daughter's bedwetting to a neighborhood parent group that met monthly with a child psychologist about everyday, normal problems. "Until I got the courage to go to that meeting, I stayed awake agonizing and reading child care books about bedwetting. They all made me feel worse. I kept the problem a secret because I worried that people would think I was a terrible parent. But one day I was too desperate to care who knew about the problem. I realized I had been centering on my feelings, not the problem."

161

After outlining her difficulty at a parent meeting, the psychologist offered Carla an explanation for her child's behavior. Explanations help us understand how our child thinks and what motivates him. In Carla's case, the explanation was one neither she nor her husband had considered. The psychologist then suggested a plan to change her child's behavior. Having a plan was like receiving a wonderful gift, says Carla.

Although we know intuitively that talking about everyday problems with family or peers helps solve problems, sometimes we need more information about child development, or we need to have someone observe our parenting and give us a reaction or a response.

When parents face a discipline dilemma, they should rule out medical causes, and once they do, these questions should be considered:

- Can I state this problem in one sentence? Most people find trying to describe a problem in one sentence difficult, but thinking about the definition helps you define clearly what troubles you about your child.
- Has this behavior become a problem for us? Time is individually defined. One parent may not want to tolerate a problem for 10 minutes; another parent lets the problem slide for months.
- Have relatives or teachers brought the problem to my attention?
- Am I continually defending my child? Do I view other people's comments as criticism of me, and do their comments anger me?

Once you answer these questions, here are additional key points to consider as you evaluate whether to seek outside advice:

162

1. Parents need to evaluate the kind of help they think they might need. Instead of advice, some parents want friends who are going through these early parenting experiences.

2. Sometimes parents need a place where they know it is "okay to say I've had it," says Dr. Eugenia Marcus, a Newton, Massachusetts pediatrician. "I don't feel I have all the answers, although I've read all the textbooks," says Marcus, the mother of two children.

3. Parents can turn to community groups for solid advice about basic questions, such as how to hire a babysitter, what toys are appropriate for a toddler, and how to teach children about music, questions that parent groups can answer.

4. In groups, parents learn about the discipline methods that work and those that do not by observing and hearing other people's experiences and attitudes.

5. Some parents encounter problems because they have a powerful need to control, yet children's behavior can make us feel powerless. Adalest-Estrin suggests, "We may need to work on overcoming our need for power, control, or influence, especially since our need may activate another powerful need: The desire to fix something."

6. Parents can, and do, make decisions without expert help. Working on a problem alone requires more time, but working on a problem with an outside expert may shorten the process.

7. Fears about admitting we have a problem burden us and prevent us from experiencing joy. We cannot solve our problems if we do not face our predicament. If you are uncomfortable talking with friends or relatives or if you believe your

problem is complex, seek professional guidance from a child psychiatrist or child psychologist. Obtain referrals from your pediatrician or from a group in the resource list at the end of this book. Get help so that you can solve the problem and free yourself to enjoy life.

QUESTIONS AND ANSWERS

Will we spoil our two-week-old infant if we keep picking her up?

No. Absolutely not. An infant who is changed and fed may need to be held, may want to suck, or just may need comfort. In later weeks, when you try to encourage your baby to sleep through the night, you may need to let her cry sometimes. Be sure she is in a safe place.

We are wondering whether we should bribe our child to go to day care or nursery school.

Forget it. Some separation anxiety is normal in young children, but you want children to attend school because they have an inner drive to learn and they enjoy being with other children. Since children aspire to act older, encourage your child by reminding him that he is acting like a big boy when he goes to school. Talk about the pleasures of learning new information. When he begins going, you can reinforce his positive behavior with a reward. Preface your offer by saying, "When you come home from day care." Do not say, "If you go." It does not matter what you offer the young child as a reward while your tone of voice tells him he is getting something wonderful for a *terrific* thing that he did. Never underestimate the power of enthusiasm, a hug and kiss, and the treat of reading one extra storybook to your child.

Our three-year-old daughter received some birthday money from her grandparents. She was impossible today; if she acts that way again we want to take away her money as a punishment. Would this be an effective way of getting her to behave?

If you decide to take away a child's money as punishment, remember that whatever you take away—even food—can become a battleground. Consider the lesson she will learn if you take away her money.

I was mortified when my three-year-old son passed along this information: Jason had used the word S--- and I explained that was a bad word. In the supermarket Jason casually observed aloud to someone on line: "You know, S--- is a bad word." Why would he do this? Should I have been more explicit?

In innocence, Jason passed on his new information because he thought it worth sharing and because, by repeating what we tell them, children reinforce the lesson. He had no idea he spoke in an inappropriate situation. Unless we explicitly inform children they cannot use the word anywhere, three-year-olds have no idea when to keep quiet. They can reasonably believe they have a choice. Even with explicit instructions, youngsters may still repeat exactly that which we would like to remain unrepeated.

Our oldest child was toilet trained by two, he spoke like an adult, and he only sucked his thumb at bedtime. When his brother was born, he began wetting his pants, talking baby talk, and sucking his thumb continuously. Why?

Expect some regression after the birth of a sibling. We sympathize because this seems alarming on the surface. But with encouragement about what older brothers can do, with emphasis on your older child's role in the family, and with positive special attention, this will pass.

A mother in my neighborhood takes preschoolers under four in her car, but does not use car seats. I keep bringing my carseat to her whenever she drives. All the other children are in seatbelts. Am I being silly or paranoid?

It is never paranoid to be safe. You may want to know that the National Highway Traffic Safety Administration guidelines suggest that from birth to nine to twelve months or 20 lbs., parents should use an infant or convertible seat facing the rear; from nine to twelve months or 20 lbs. to four years or 40 lbs., use a convertible or toddler seat. You should check with your state, since laws vary from state to state. Some states say children between one and four sitting in the front of the car must be in a child restraint; if they sit in the rear, then children between one and four may be buckled into regular car seat belts or a child restraint.

My mother takes care of our young daughter, but she and I disagree over some discipline approaches. I don't know how to handle this difference of opinion, especially since she is doing me a favor. What can I do?

Parents must include the primary caregivers in discussions about discipline since consistency about discipline is important. If this caregiver is a relative, obviously it is harder. When you hire someone, queries about discipline approaches should be one of your interview questions. Consider whether your discipline problem with your mother is really one of guilt about leaving your child. After thinking it through, first talk with your mother and try to come up with an approach both of you can live with. If you cannot reach agreement, you need to decide if can live with the difference or look for different child care.

I have noticed my toddler masturbating more often and in inappropriate situations. Is this abnormal? Should I punish him? How should I react?

Children are not thinking adult thoughts when they explore their bodies. Masturbation is normal in children when they discover that manipulation of their genitalia can cause a pleasurable sensation. Discipline in this instance consists of teaching them when this exploration is inappropriate. You can explain to your child that it is okay to touch himself, but it is not polite to do this in public. Children are understandably curious about their bodies; you may find them exploring each other's bodies. If you make a fuss about this and overreact and punish the child, you will make your child feel uncomfortable about his body. It is important not to overreact. If masturbation seems excessive or if you are concerned, discuss it with your pediatrician.

GLOSSARY

ADD Attention deficit disorder, a medical disorder characterized by poor attention span and distractibility with or without hyperactivity.

Assertive When you clearly and firmly state what you believe or feel, you give an impression of control and decisiveness without emotional overtones.

Attachment As a positive statement, attachment can be a strong and affectionate bond; as a negative statement attachment can mean unwillingness to be independent.

Boundaries Specific restrictions that we place on children; for example, "You can walk to the curb, but not beyond," or "You must drink your milk at the table."

Botulism An extremely severe case of food poisoning produced by a substance found in improperly canned or preserved food that can poison or destroy nerve tissue.

Consequences The results of an action and the point of discipline: to teach children that behavior has positive and negative outcomes.

Consistent The act of steadily maintaining a disciplinary course of action over a period of time.

Developmental Progressive and continuous changes that begin to occur in children from the moment they are born. The ages and stages of child development vary greatly, and sometimes family patterns are noticed.

Discipline A series of acts serving to guide your children to appropriate behavior and the understanding that their actions affect themselves and others.

Feedback   Information given by parents in response to a child's actions.

Independent   The goal of discipline is to help children think or act for themselves.

Infants   The period of time from birth to about 10 months.

Negotiation   Discussions with your child that lead to an agreement and course of action.

Pediatrician   A medical doctor who specializes in the care and treatment of children.

Psychiatrist   A medical doctor who specializes in mental health.

Psychologist   A specialist in mind and behavior with either a master's or doctorate degree.

Punishment   A negative form of discipline involving a penalty.

Spoil   The result of not disciplining children, which leads to youngsters who focus on their needs only.

Time-out   A discipline technique during which your child is removed from an activity or source of conflict to provide time for reflection and calming.

Toddler   A period from roughly 10 months to 2 years old.

RESOURCES FOR PARENTS

Alcohol, Drug Abuse and Mental Health Administration
5600 Fishers Lane
Rockville, MD 20857
1-301-443-3783

Besides information on substance abuse, this agency publishes pamphlets on such subjects as the importance of play, and preterm babies. It also sponsors research on such topics as infant development and mother-child bonding.

American Academy of Pediatrics (AAP)
P.O. Box 927
Elk Grove Village, IL 60009-0927
708-228-5005

The AAP publishes useful, inexpensive pamphlets on such topics as first aid and child restraint systems. Most are available free when accompanied by a self-addressed envelope. A publication catalog, *Parents Resource Guide*, is available; it lists information and pamphlets. The AAP prefers written inquiries and offers a pediatrician and referral service by geography or by specialty in that region. Send a self-addressed stamped envelope. For any request, mark Dept. C on the envelope and the request.

American Self-Help Clearinghouse
St. Clare's–Riverside Medical Center
Denville, NJ 07834
201-625-7501
201-625-9053 (TDD)

The Clearinghouse publishes a directory; it will refer you to local self-help clearinghouses and help people start self-help groups.

Association for Childhood Education International (ACEI)
11501 Georgia Ave., Suite 315
Wheaton, MD 20902
301-942-2443

This 100-year-old professional organization deals with children's development, care, and well-being from infancy through early adolescence. It publishes numerous publications, including the *Childhood Education* journal five times a year, offering feature articles on educational trends and theory, research, and reviews of professional and children's books, videos, and classroom software. Write for information.

Consumer Product Safety Commission (CPSC)
Washington, DC 20207
Toll-free hotline: (800) 638-CPSC, 8:30 a.m. to 5 p.m. EST, weekdays

Call to report product-related complaints or injuries or to check on equipment safety. The CPSC deals with safety standards for cribs, toys, bikes, and other childhood paraphernalia and will provide guidelines for choosing safe toys and making your home child-proof. This agency also publishes some important pamphlets. For a complete list, write to the above address; place the publication request at top.

Family Resource Coalition
200 S. Michigan, Suite 1520
Chicago, IL 60604
312-341-9361

The Coalition is currently compiling a computerized family support service directory to use for professional referrals or for parents if they want to start groups in their communities. The FRC also has a four-page fact sheet to help parents systematically search for information on parenting services.

La Leche League International
9616 Minneapolis Ave.
Franklin Park, IL 60131
Tel. 1-LALECHE, 9 a.m. to 3 p.m. CST, or 708-455-7730, 8 a.m. to 4 p.m. CST; after hours you will get a number for a volunteer leader.

La Leche publishes numerous pamphlets, books, and a newsletter, which are made available to nonmembers. There are chapters in virtually every U.S. area. Consult your local phone book or call the main office. Trained volunteers answer phone questions and sometimes make house calls to help new nursing mothers with problems; they have access to expert advice on lactation and breast-feeding.

National Association of Mothers' Centers
336 Fulton Ave.
Hempstead, NY 11550
516-486-6614 or 800-645-3828

These are groups that meet for 90 minutes weekly in 8- to 10-week cycles guided by two trained center members. Child care is available during group times.

173

National Poison Center Network
3705 Fifth Ave. at DeSoto Street
Pittsburgh, PA 15213
412-681-6669 for poison emergency or drug and poison information
412-692-5315 for educational materials

Call information for the poison center in your area. The network offers home poison control materials, including poison plant lists and "Mr. Yuk" stickers. Write for current prices, which are low.

SUGGESTED READINGS

Brenner, Barbara. *Love and Discipline* (Ballantine, 1983).

Faber, Adele, and Mazlish, Elaine. *How to Talk So Kids Will Listen & Listen So Kids Will Talk* (Avon Books, 1980).

Ferber, Richard, M.D. *Solve Your Child's Sleep Problems* (Simon & Schuster, 1985).

Fraiberg, Selma. *The Magic Years* (Scribners, paperback classic first written in 1959).

Hausner, Lee, Ph.D. *Children of Paradise* (Jeremy P. Tarcher, Inc., 1990).

Leach, Penelope. *Your Growing Child, From Babyhood Through Adolescence* (Alfred A. Knopf, 1990).

Leftin, Howard I., M.D. *The Family Contract, A Blueprint for Successful Parenting* (PIA Press, 1990).

Lovejoy, Frederick H., Jr. M.D., Medical Editor, and Estridge, David, Executive Editor. *Boston Children's Hospital, The New Child Health Encyclopedia, The Complete Guide for Parents* (Dell, 1987).

Mendler, Allen N., Ph.D. *Smiling at Yourself, Educating Young Children About Stress and Self-Esteem* (Network Publications, A Division of ETR Associates, 1990).

Schmitt, Barton D., M.D., F.A.A.P. *Your Child's Health, The Parents' Guide to Symptoms, Emergencies, Common Illnesses, Behavior, and School Problems* (Bantam Books, 1991).

Shelov, Steven, M.D., F.A.A.P., Editor-in-Chief, and Robert E. Hannemann, M.D., F.A.A.P., Associate Medical

Editor. *The American Academy of Pediatrics, Caring For Your Baby and Young Child, Birth to Age 5, The Complete and Authoritative Guide* (Bantam Books, 1991).

Starer, Daniel. *Who to Call—The Parent's Source Book* (William Morrow, 1992).

Van Pelt, Katie. *A Practical Guide for Easier Toilet Training, Potty Training Your Baby* (Avery Publishing Group, 1988).

INDEX

Acting out, 47
Activity transitions, 19, 117
Adalest-Estrin, Ann, 161, 163
Advice, seeking, 160–164
Aggressive child, 143–147
Anderson, Daniel, 148, 150
Angry parents, 77
Answering back, 110–114
Apologizing to a child, 106–109
Appetite, 129
Appropriate behavior, 80, 111
Approval, 92
Assertiveness, 17

Bargaining, 107
Bartoshuk, Linda, 128
Battles of will, 18
Bedtime resistance
    progressive delay
        method for, 50–51
    reasons for, 50
    sharing parental bed
        and, 52

tips for parents, 52–53
Behavior
    appropriate, 80, 111
    ignoring, 18
    misbehavior, 74
    normal, 74
    standards of, 14–15, 76–79
    unwanted, 103
Berenstain Bears, The
    (Berenstain), 63
Berenstain, Jan, 63
Berenstain, Stan, 63
Body language, 31
Bribes, 80–84, 165
Business calls, 96

Car seats, 167
Children's Minds
    (Donaldson), 141
Children Under Pressure
    (Heffernan), 122
Choosing battles, 69
Chores, 62–66
Christophersen, Edward, 20
Clean-up chores, 62–66
Commercials (TV), 131

Communication, parental, 8–9
Company manners, 76–79
Competition, 90
Consequences, 13–14, 17–18, 73
Considerate behavior, 89–92
Constructive discipline, 67–70
Contemporary Pediatrics, 137
Cooper, Kenneth, 130
Cooperation, 62–66, 89, 132–135
Corporal punishment, 10–15
Curse words, 54–57, 166

Dawdling, 115–118
Daydreaming, 117
Destructive discipline, 67–70
Dietz, William, 149
Different rules, 6–9, 102–105, 167
Difficult child, 58–61
Disapproval, 74
Discipline
  destructive v. constructive, 67–70
  disagreements over, 6–9, 167
  effective, 4
  failure of, 58–61
  for ill child, 136–139
  strategy for, 4–5
Distraction, 14, 101
Dobson, James, 3
Doctors, 158
Donaldson, Margaret, 141

Effective discipline, 4
Embarrassment in public, 71–75
Emergency 911 training, 94–95, 96
Empathy, 89–92
Engel, Nancy, 6, 8
Exercise, 130
Exhaustion, parental, 152–155
Experts, 156–159

Faber, Adele, 84, 125
Family rule, 104
Fantasy play, 119–120
Fast food, 130
Feedback, 81
  positive, 82, 153
Ferber, Richard, 50
Fighting with friends or siblings, 46–49
Food preferences, 128–131
Forbes, David, 119–120
Forgetfulness, 115–118
Free to Be You (record), 100, 131
Friendships, 119–120
  stages of, 121

tips for parents,
121–123
Fry, William, 155

Games, 135
Gerbner, George, 149
Good habits, 62–66
Grandparents, 159
Guest responsibilities,
76–79

Healthy snacks, 131
Heffernan, Helen, 122
Help, outside, 160–164
*How to Talk So Kids
Will Listen & Listen
So Kids Will Talk*
(Faber & Mazlish),
84, 125
Humor, 70, 155

Illness, 136–139
Impulse control, 113
Inconsistency, 74
Individuality, 67
Insensitivity, 89–92
Interactive toys, 150
Isolated child, 121

Judgmental comments, 92

Kid Fitness (Cooper), 130
Kindness, 90–91

Language, 29
crude, 54–57

Leach, Penelope, 129
Limits, 78
Listening to child, 30–31
Literalness, 140–141
Lying, 39–40
reasons for, 38
tips for parents, 41

Manners, 77, 92, 124
technique for child's
cooperation, 125
tips for parents,
126–127
Masturbation, 168
Mazlish, Elaine, 84, 125
"Mean world syndrome,"
149
Medium tasters, 128
Mendler, Allan, 56, 92
Messy Room (Berenstain),
63
Misbehavior, 74

Name calling, 54–57
New York Times, 105
Nontasters, 128

Obstinate children, 59
O'Malley, Julie, 18, 140
Open-ended questions, 68
Organizational skills, 116
Outside help, 160–164
Overscheduling, 122
Overstimulation, 61

Pacifiers, 21–24

Parental communication, 8–9

Parental exhaustion, 152–155

Passive child, 143–147

Physical exercise, 47

Physical punishment, 10–15

Playgroups, 120

Potty, 35

Power struggle, 106

Privacy, 140–142

Problem-solving skills, 29–32

Problem-Solving Techniques in Childrearing (Spivak), 31, 31–32

Procaccini, Joseph, 157

Progressive delay method, 50–51

Public embarrassment, 71–75

Public tantrums, 27

Punishments, 166
    time out, 16, 18, 20

Refereeing fights, 49

Regression, 166–167

Resources for parents, 171–174

Respect, 77, 106–109

Reusser, Jonathan, 153–154

Rewards, 92

distinguished from bribes, 80–83

tips for parents, 83–84

Rivalry, sibling, 85–88

Rules, differing, 6–9, 102–105, 167

Schmitt, Barton, 127, 129, 136–137

Schure, Myrna, 31–32

Security, 91

Security objects, 21–24

Self-esteem, 68, 82, 88, 90

Selman, Robert, 121

Sharing, 132–135

Shopping trips, 98–101

Sibling fights, 46–49

Sibling rivalry, 85–88

Sick child, 136–139

Small choices, 18

Smiling at Yourself, Educating Young Children About Stress and Self-esteem (Mendler), 56

Social skills, 119–123

Spanking, 10–15, 67–68

Spilling liquids, 69

Spivak, George, 31–32

Spoiled child, 137, 165

Stealing, 42–45

Supermarket trips, 98–101

Supertasters, 128

Support groups, 161

Sweets, 130